100 Ideas for Teaching Personal, Social and Emotional Development

Continuum 100 Ideas for the Early Years Series

100 Ideas for Teaching Communication, Language and Literacy –
   Susan Elkin

100 Ideas for Teaching Creative Development – Wendy Bowkett and
   Stephen Bowkett

100 Ideas for Teaching Knowledge and Understanding of the World –
   Alan Thwaites

100 Ideas for Teaching Personal, Social and Emotional Development –
   Judith Thwaites

100 Ideas for Teaching Physical Development – Simon Brownhill

100 Ideas for Teaching Problem Solving, Reasoning and Numeracy –
   Alan Thwaites

Continuum One Hundreds Series

100+ Ideas for Managing Behaviour – Johnnie Young

100+ Ideas for Teaching Creativity – Stephen Bowkett

100+ Ideas for Teaching Thinking Skills – Stephen Bowkett

100 Ideas for Supply Teachers: Primary School Edition – Michael Parry

100 Ideas for Essential Teaching Skills – Neal Watkin and Johannes Ahrenfelt

100 Ideas for Assemblies: Primary School Edition – Fred Sedgwick

100 Ideas for Lesson Planning – Anthony Haynes

100 Ideas for Teaching

Personal, Social and Emotional Development

Judith Thwaites

continuum

Continuum International Publishing Group

The Tower Building
11 York Road
SE1 7NX

80 Maiden Lane
Suite 704
New York, NY 10038

www.continuumbooks.com

British Library Cataloguing-in-Publication Data
A catalogue record for this book is available from the British Library.

ISBN: 9781847063823 (paperback)

Library of Congress Cataloging-in-Publication Data
A catalog record for this book is available from the Library of Congress.

Illustrations by Kerry Ingham

Typeset by Ben Cracknell Studios | www.benstudios.co.uk
Printed and bound in Great Britain by Cromwell Press, Wiltshire

Contents

Acknowledgements

Thank you to Alan Thwaites for his patience and support and for proofreading.

Grateful thanks also to Penny Tassoni, who made this book possible.

Reference
Every Child Matters, the Statutory Framework for the Early Years Foundation
Stage (EYFS), is available as a download from www.standards.dfes.gov.uk/eyfs/

Introduction

Positive influences and experiences in their early years give children the best possible foundation for their journey through life, helping them towards achieving personal, social and emotional health. Having their emotional needs met and knowing they are special, gradually brings about children's self-esteem and self-confidence – vital for coping with relationships and, not least, for caring about themselves.

Guidelines for the provision of care for the 0 to 5 years age group have been brought together by the DfES (now DCFS) in the 2007 Statutory Framework for the Early Years Foundation Stage (EYFS). Outlining the requisite skills, attitudes and knowledge for this age group, the Framework also sets out guidelines for the kind of experiences that should be incorporated into daily routines in order to target those skills. The activities suggested in the Framework should enable children to learn with enjoyment and at their own pace.

By their very nature, many of the elements of the Personal, Social and Emotional Development (PSED) area of the Framework are already inherent in the other five EYFS areas of learning, namely: Communication, Language and Literacy; Problem Solving, Reasoning and Numeracy; Knowledge and Understanding of the World; Physical Development; and Creative Development. Important skills such as forming relationships, sharing, turn-taking and self-control are addressed and strengthened by sound practice right across the board, as are, of course, attitudes towards gender, social, cultural and physical equality.

The ongoing process of becoming balanced and whole individuals in the early years forms the basis for the PSED area of the EYFS Framework. The PSED area is subdivided into six aspects, listed below with a brief description of what each one is about.

Dispositions and Attitudes
- Seeing oneself as separate and special.
- Expressing own likes, dislikes and preferences.
- Developing independence and self-belief.
- Feeling comfortable with trying unfamiliar activities.
- Being motivated to persevere.

Self-confidence and Self-esteem
- Feeling emotionally safe within relationships with key people.
- Having the confidence to express feelings, to explore and to attempt challenges.
- Seeking to be looked at and approved of.

Making Relationships
- Interacting happily with adults and other children.
- Learning to be flexible to allow for the needs of others.
- Waiting, sharing, turn-taking, and understanding that there are certain agreed codes of behaviour.
- Valuing and taking care of own well-being.

Behaviour and Self-control
- Adapting to routine events, and responding to some simple behavioural expectations.
- Learning to show care for other people, for living things and the environment, with a growing awareness of the potential effects of words and actions on others.

Self-care
- Communicating needs and expressing preferences.
- Showing interest in food routines.
- Enjoying increasing independence in relation to personal care and hygiene.
- Feeling a sense of pride in own achievements.

Sense of Community
- Having a positive self-image.
- Learning that physical and other differences and similarities link and distinguish them from others.
- Joining in with family routines and traditional events.
- Recognizing people and places from different areas of their own lives.

Using this book
This book is intended for all those caring for children who are seeking a fund of simple, practical ideas, particularly those wanting to enhance the personal, social and emotional development of the children in their care. The ideas are specially selected to be enjoyable, and fun to do with the children over and over again. Feel free to adapt and/or repeat a selection of the ideas regularly. Children find routines a comfort, and gain confidence in their own general abilities once some independence has been established through repetition.

Since each of the 100 ideas addresses more than one aspect of the Framework, it has been most practical to divide the book into sections based on age bands rather than on the aspects themselves. These six age bands, which are fairly broad and which also overlap, are taken directly from the EYFS age bands which apply to all subject areas. Since so much development takes place between birth and five years, the built-in overlap between consecutive age bands allows for variations in children's rates of development. Naturally, many of the ideas in this book can be easily and successfully adapted to suit age groups other than the ones suggested.

How the ideas are set out
Group size
Most of the suggestions for group size are flexible, for example 'Any' is common, as is 'Small', although 'Individual' is really most effective with just one baby or child.

Focus
The EYFS aspects predominantly covered by each idea are set out under the heading 'Focus'.

Preparation/Resources
Preparation time for each idea is minimal, and the ideas generally require simple, already available resources.

Taking this further
You will obviously draw on your own experience to adapt and innovate, but where considered useful, a few tried and tested extensions or further ideas are added under this heading.

Safety note
Occasionally I have flagged up what I consider to be the main pitfalls with regard to health and safety, but appreciate that you know your children and can best predict what they are capable of doing.

And finally . . .
Help children to learn positively from their mistakes and to understand that 'failure' can genuinely be useful. Praise and encourage, even if an attempt has been unsuccessful. If we can provide children with a wealth of opportunities to form close relationships and show them how to interact with others, as well as to enjoy playing alone; and if we help them work out strategies to cope, showing them how effective these can be for ourselves; if we listen to children carefully and show them by our example how to *want* to listen to others, then we provide the

best possible experiences to help children feel strong and positive about themselves.

Because children can seem like sponges, mirrors and echoes all rolled into one, the role played by key people in setting a good example and in providing the best early years experiences is clear – it is one of great responsibility and privilege.

SECTION 1 — Birth –11 months

While generally happy to be looked after by anyone who is competent, warm and caring, newborn and very young babies already show a preference for their most familiar carers, recognizing them by voice and 'smell'.

By three months, babies respond clearly to attention and praise, listening intently to the voice of someone close to their faces and communicating their pleasure by smiling, gurgling, wriggling and waving arms and legs enthusiastically.

By six months babies are able to communicate expressions of anger, anxiety or annoyance, but are very social and love seeing new people. Soon after this age, though, they may seem anxious around strangers or about certain situations, often becoming attached almost exclusively to a key person. Especially at this time, their lives should be as routine as possible; their sense of security comes largely from being able to anticipate what happens next.

Towards the end of this stage, babies start to 'chomp at the bit', eager to be more grown up and independent. They usually want to take over feeding and undressing or dressing themselves, and start to mimic grown-up activities such as washing up or cooking. They are 'into everything' and can be headstrong, quite vocally expressing frustration when thwarted.

IDEA

1

Snug as a Bug

Focus	Group size	Preparation/Resources
Self-confidence and Self-esteem	Individual	A light baby blanket or wrap
Behaviour and Self-control		

Babies gain physical, psychological and emotional comfort from 'snuggling in' with a familiar adult in a secure setting.

- With the baby's limbs loosely contained in the blanket, cradle the baby in your arms or lay her/him on your lap facing you.
- Make a little joke of popping out one arm or a leg in turn, each time saying, 'Oooh! Put it away!' Wrap the baby up again, sometimes giving a little hug or gently rubbing a shoulder through the blanket to emphasize the security of being warm and cuddled.
- Make plenty of eye contact, smile, keep talking and use the baby's name in a warm tone of voice.

Safety note
Avoid cellular blankets for this game in case small fingers become caught in the holes.

Baby Chat

Focus	Group size	Preparation/Resources
Dispositions and Attitudes	Individual	None
Self-confidence and Self-esteem		
Making Relationships		

This activity can be started with very young babies, who are comforted by the voices of familiar carers and love receiving their undivided attention.

- Choose a time when the baby is comfortable and alert. With the baby cradled in your arms or lying down in front of you, say or sing a personalized rhyme, gently touching the baby's nose, fingers, feet, hands or toes.
- Say any words that pop into your head (example below), or make up the words and borrow the tune from a nursery rhyme, as in the second example:

[Jody's] nose	Or:	(to the tune of 'Polly put the kettle on',
[Jody's] toes		sing while completing a nappy change)
I like this toe		*[Mandy] put the nappy on* (three times)
Where did it go?		*You're all clean and dry.* (gently pat the
(make a toe disappear		nappy)
under the baby		*[Rosie] waved her legs about* (three times,
blanket or wrap, then		gently 'cycling' the baby's legs in the air)
feign surprise when it		*She's all tired now!* (blow out your own
reappears)		cheeks)

- Maintain the 'conversation' by responding positively to all the baby's communications and gestures, and build on them. Use the baby's name frequently.

Taking this further

Match the baby's two eyes, one nose, lots of wiggly fingers, and so on, with your own, naming the owner and the body parts each time.

IDEA

3

Catch a Baby

Focus	Group size	Preparation/Resources
Dispositions and Attitudes	Individual	Cot blanket or large towel
Self-confidence and Self-esteem		
Making Relationships		
Behaviour and Self-control		

This game helps babies to understand that they are 'separate'. It also provides another excuse for a cuddle, giving security and comfort.

- Lay the baby in the middle of a blanket in a safe place on the floor. Position yourself a short distance away. Wave to the baby, and say, 'Hello [Davey]! What are you doing over there? Come back here! Here comes [Davey]' Then, gently pulling the blanket at two corners, carefully slide the baby towards you.
- Pick the baby up and have a cuddle.
- Repeat one or more times, for as long as it's still enjoyable for the baby.

Safety note

If the baby is able to roll over from her or his back, this game is best played in a safe place on the floor rather than on a raised surface.

Taking this further

Try absenting yourself for brief moments by sitting on the floor with your back to the baby in the bouncy chair, then swivelling round and softly saying, 'Boo!' with a welcoming smile, or play the classic 'Peek-a-boo' game with a cushion.

Bits and Bobs

Focus	Group size	Preparation/Resources
Making Relationships	Individual	None
Behaviour and Self-control		

As well as enjoying a quality time 'chat' with trusted people, babies are comforted by familiar routines and frequently repeated words such as action rhymes.

When the baby is clean, fed and alert, enjoy an action rhyme together. Here are three ideas – the first is an example of a made-up rhyme, followed by two traditional ones that also work well.

Eyes open, (stretch your own eyes wide open, while gently pointing to the baby's eyes from the side)
Nose beeps, (say 'Beep-beep' while pressing nose)
Smiley mouth, (gently pull up corners of baby's mouth and you smile too)
Rosy cheeks. (rub cheeks)
Yummy yummy, round tummy. (rub tummy round and round)
Two knees, (touch both)
Ten toes, (gently rub along them or count each one)
Nibble nibble,
Eat those! (pretend to be about to take a mouthful, or to nibble the toes)

Round and round the garden, like a teddy bear, (circle your index finger round the baby's palm)
One step, two step, (jump finger up same arm)
Tickle you under there! (gently tickle under the arm)

Knock on the door, (gently tap the baby's forehead)
Peep in the windows, (look smilingly into the eyes)
Lift the latch, (gently push up the end of the baby's nose)
Walk in. (walk two fingers up the baby's chin onto the bottom lip)

Baby Weather Watch

Focus	Group size	Preparation/Resources
All six aspects	Individual	No special preparations

This simple idea encourages an awareness of different types of weather, and enjoyment of the elements.

Next time it rains, snows, blows or the sun shines warmly and you are taking care of a baby, dress the baby up according to the weather and go out to enjoy it together – ideas below.

- Rain – holding the baby facing outwards, show wonder and excitement at the raindrops. While babies at this stage may be too young to have their own wellies, the next best thing is to be held by you as you jump and splash in the puddles.
- Snow – chat about the snow that's falling, and the snow already on the ground, using vocabulary such as 'soft'/'cold'/'scrunch'. Make sure the baby feels the sensations of snow before drying out and warming up thoroughly indoors.
- Wind – take a piece of material outside with you and let it wave and flap about, keeping it well away from faces. Pretend to be blown around by the wind while holding the baby. Watch the leaves blowing 'round and round'.
- Sun – young or old, we all feel cheered by sunshine. It's lovely in the shade of trees too, and (suitably sun-protected) babies can cool off with a little bowl of water, a new, clean paint brush and a bit of help to daub cool water onto their feet or knees, or be fanned with a folded sheet of paper.

Safety note

Be sure not to let the baby look directly into the sun.

It's in the Bag

Focus	Group size	Preparation/Resources
Making Relationships Sense of Community	Individual	Baby toys/baby-safe items Large, woven stand-up bag, such as those sold at supermarket checkouts

This game involves the baby in the anticipation and pleasure of discovery – in this case, of what's hiding in the bag.

- Place a number of objects (such as toys/wooden spoon/baby shoe) in the bag, giving consideration to the baby's normal attention span to help decide on quantity and choice of objects.
- With the baby sitting in front of you (in a baby chair or bouncing cradle), take out one item at a time and talk about it. Operate any moving parts/sounds then give it to the baby to feel or hold. Provide a running commentary using the baby's name all the time.
- As the baby finishes with each object, replace it in the bag with all the other treasures. Occasionally, instead of a fresh object, whip out one that the baby has already seen. Watch for signs of recognition.
- After the game the baby can help you tip out the contents of the bag and play with whichever item appeals.

IDEA 7

Just Pop This On

Focus	Group size	Preparation/Resources
Dispositions and Attitudes Self-confidence and Self-esteem Making Relationships Behaviour and Self-control Sense of Community	Individual	One of the baby's clean sleep suits

This is all about enjoying quality time together.

- At bath or changing time, and with the baby alert and happy, add a sound effect to the undoing or the doing up of each sleep suit popper, for example:

   (undoing) Ping! Kkkk! Blop! Rrrrr! Ding! Ouch!
   (doing up) Aaah! Pop! Mmmm! Woooh! Hahaa!

- Before placing a foot or hand into the sleep suit, gently 'wibble-wobble' the baby's leg or arm around and make a big deal of trying to catch it to put in the hole.
- Push your hand right through an empty sleeve, from cuff towards shoulder end, then wiggle your fingers about saying, 'Where's [Jon-Jon's] hand . . . ah, there it is!' before gently grabbing the baby's hand and pulling it down through the sleeve to come through the correct end. If you know each other well, blow a raspberry on the baby's fist when it appears, or pretend to eat it. Repeat for the other sleeve if the baby liked it the first time.

Sleep suits are great and are made from stretchy fabric, so the possibilities are limited only by your imagination. Older babies appreciate jokes such as putting a small soft toy in the sleeve so it pops out when their arm is put in the sleeve; or you could do all the poppers up while the baby has her/his arms around the waist, so sleeves can be flapped about empty.

Water Music

Focus	Group size	Preparation/Resources
Dispositions and Attitudes	Individual or small	4 or 5 coloured or pretty glasses, or plain glasses and food colouring in the water (thinner glass is more effective than thick, tumbler-style glass)
Self-confidence and Self-esteem		
Making Relationships		
Behaviour and Self-control		Clean water
Sense of Community		Pencil, or wooden spoon

Enjoy a special moment with the baby as you create a musical and visual display.

- Place the glasses in a row, if possible on a sunny, accessible windowsill, with varying amounts of coloured or plain water in each glass; this looks lovely with the sun reflecting on the glasses. Alternatively, use a table top.
- Test the 'notes' by tapping the outside of each glass near the rim with the handle of the wooden spoon or the pencil. Add or remove water to obtain a pleasing mix of different sounds.
- Let the baby see you gently tap each glass, and listen together to the magical ringing sound that is made.
- Even if you're not musical, sing the notes and the baby will definitely appreciate it.
- 'Play' several notes in succession, then if you feel confident, build up into a known or made-up little tune which you can sing words, hum or 'la' along to.
- Guide the baby's hand gently to tap the glasses with the spoon handle and produce some sounds.

Safety note

Use anti-slip plastic matting if necessary to hold the glasses firmly.

Hold the baby throughout.

Clear the glasses away at the end of the activity to remove the chance of accidents.

IDEA 9

Eye on the Ball

Focus	Group size	Preparation/Resources
Dispositions and Attitudes Self-confidence and Self-esteem Making Relationships Sense of Community	Individual	Clean, colourful, baby-safe ball

Babies love to see the bright, moving ball during this interactive game.

- With the baby sitting or lying comfortably in front of you, perhaps in a bouncing cradle, keep the ball moving to attract her/his attention, for example:
    - Spin the ball on your finger.
    - Throw and catch it a little way in the air, smacking your hands on it to make a satisfying noise as you catch it.
    - Roll it down your arm.
    - Balance it on your head.
    - Play peep-bo with it.
- Constantly chat to the baby by name, responding to any body language or sounds she or he makes.
- Involving the baby more once you have her/his attention, roll the ball slowly up the baby's leg, then gently round the tummy.
- If appropriate for the age, gently place the baby's hands on the ball and hold them there for a moment so that she/he can feel the ball. Keep talking about what's going on with the ball and with the baby.
- Make the ball disappear briefly behind you or behind the bouncing cradle, bringing it back enthusiastically.

IDEA 10

Hokey Cokey for Babies

Focus	Group size	Preparation/Resources
Self-care	Individual	Baby's coat or jacket

This idea involves babies in their own personal care at the simplest level – beginning to help with dressing themselves.

- When putting on a coat or jacket, hold the baby's hand and gently guide it in and out of the arm hole, then gently shake the arm while singing 'in-out, in-out and shake it all about', then – 'IN!' Complete putting on the coat, inserting the tricky second arm yourself.
- Repeat on other days, alternating right/left arm first.
- Over days and weeks, gradually offer the correct end of the sleeve, prompting the baby to place her or his own hand into the coat sleeve.

Taking this further

If the baby is holding a small object in the hand, make a game of it going through the sleeve like a train through a tunnel and coming out at the other end.

IDEA 11

See the Signs

Focus	Group size	Preparation/Resources
All six aspects	Small or individual	Familiarity with the signs used by children in your care

There is growing evidence that small children who are able to convey some of their needs through 'signing' with their hands are more likely to avoid frustration than a child who has a less direct means of communication. If you are interested in finding out more to help you make up your mind about signing, there is plenty of information in publications as well as on the internet. Many people believe that learning to sign actually enhances a child's language development in the long term.

Baby signing is intended to be fun, and never stressful for the child or carer.

- Around seven or eight months is a good time to start teaching a baby to sign, but you can successfully start later. It's fine to make up your own versions of the hand signs, but you may wish to find out which signs, if any, are already used by the children in your care and continue with these where possible.
- Use signs at the appropriate time, such as 'sleep' at nap time; 'milk' when about to give a bottle. Make the sign and say the word clearly, being consistent in the situation, sign and word that you use. Different children may take anything from a few weeks to months to be able to reproduce the sign in the right context, but your patience will be rewarded. If the process seems to be taking a long time, remember that everything is 'going in' meanwhile.
- If the baby signs differently or incorrectly, calmly repeat the sign and word. Gently shape the baby's hand with your fingers to help make the required sign.
- Babies may eventually develop a working knowledge of dozens of different signs and be able to 'chat' with their carer about why they are crying or what they need. The following sign-able words relate to some basic needs, which babies definitely appreciate having sorted out without too much delay: Mummy/Daddy/sleep/thirsty/nappy/juice/milk/hungry/hurt/tummy-ache/hot/cold/more/no/yes/happy.

Note that most of the signs can be used by both carer ('asking') and baby ('telling') in conversation, to establish what the baby needs.

And So To Bed

Focus	Group size	Preparation/Resources
Behaviour and Self-control	Individual	CD or tape player and selection of relaxing music

Babies who spend their day in a care setting are comforted by the familiarity of the routines carried out by caring and consistent adults. Nap times can be made especially peaceful and soothing with the regular addition of some well-chosen background music or sounds.

- At snuggle time or nap time, play CDs of gentle music at low volume. Many Mozart and Vivaldi tracks are especially harmonious and calming, or you could use any easy-listening music. Try also music for healing, e.g. Reiki – either instrumental or natural sounds.
- Holding the baby quite closely, gently sway and dip to the rhythm and sing or hum softly to the music.
- Walk around very slowly, pausing at the window/in front of a picture or the baby's cot, chatting quietly. Cuddle the baby until she/he feels secure and relaxed when put down to sleep.

Making the routine simple and as unchanging as possible means that even if the carer changes from day to day, the routine will always be familiar. Provided regularly, this cosy routine will be cherished and looked forward to by the babies.

SECTION 2

8 – 20 months

As babies' mobility and confidence develop they follow the urge to explore and to discover how things work, finding that they can influence people and events around them. Their range of emotions grows wider and more complex as the need for being constantly at the side of their main carer jostles with a quest for independence and a great curiosity. They can be very demonstrative, giving special people enthusiastic cuddles and kisses.

There is no concept of danger, nor understanding yet of having to wait for, or being denied, something. They do not relate to yesterday and tomorrow or past and future.

During this stage, a baby's sense of humour emerges and they may laugh quite infectiously at a funny action or sound.

By the end of this stage, spoken vocabulary is increasing, although toddlers still understand very much more than they can articulate.

Hide and Speak

Focus	Group size	Preparation/Resources
Self-confidence and Self-esteem	Individual or	None
Making Relationships	small	
Behaviour and Self-control		

This activity becomes increasingly two-way as the baby develops more sophisticated ways of communicating.

With the baby lying, or sitting propped up in front of you, cover your own eyes with your hands or a small cushion, then ask a series of questions, each time removing your hands or cushion and showing mock surprise and pleasure or giving a little cuddle or squeeze, as appropriate. For example:

'Where are you, [Joey]?' (when the baby responds with a sound or gesture) 'Oh, there you are!' (give a warm smile and a little hug)

Further questions to ask:

- 'Have you got your shoes on?'
- 'Is Teddy there?'
- 'Can Teddy bounce on your tummy/stand on his head/jump over you/beep your nose?' (animate the cuddly toy)
- 'Have you drunk up all your milk?'
- 'Where are [Joey's] fingers/toes?'
- 'Where's your nose?'

Although you will mostly find yourself answering your own questions, remember always to maintain the 'conversation' by responding positively to the baby's gurgles, squeaks and waving arms and legs.

IDEA

14

Building Bridges

Focus	Group size	Preparation/Resources
All six aspects	Small	Set of wooden bricks
		Clean kitchen-roll tubes (optional)

This helps to build the children's positive self-image, making the most of a little quality time between children and carer.

- Guide the babies as they use the bricks to build:
    - a tower
    - a bridge (flattened kitchen-roll tubes can form the span)
    - parking bays or a garage for toy cars
    - a bed for a small doll (add a 'blanket' such as a piece of soft material)
    - a few steps for a toy figure to climb before jumping off onto a cushion, then bouncing off as from a trampoline
    - an enclosure for toy sheep
    - a play park.
- Using the babies' ideas as far as possible, support just enough to ensure success. Admire and praise all efforts and have older children or adults come over to view the models as well.

IDEA 15

Important Little Steps

Focus	Group size	Preparation/Resources
Dispositions and Attitudes Self-confidence and Self-esteem	1 or 2	Cuddly toy(s) Small blanket(s) Simple toys or child-safe objects that will stack, or are graduated in size, e.g. plastic cups/different sized spoons/rigid gift boxes with lids firmly attached

When very young children achieve new skills in the course of a day they are spurred on by the delight and enthusiasm of their carers. This idea outlines a variety of extra skills to teach babies, so that they can experience the same success and adult approval.

Teach babies to:

- pat-a-cake (clap hands together)
- move one hand in a circle in the air to denote circular movement every time you spot something together that goes round and round (cot mobile/ washing machine/toy car wheels/clock hand) or when you sing 'Wheels on the bus'
- cover a cuddly toy with a blanket and kiss it on the head, saying, 'Goodnight' or 'Sleep tight' or whatever is familiar to the children, then tiptoe away. This action can feel very grown up to a small child and encourages taking responsibility for a friend
- play 'Copycat'. Stack or line up the toys or plastic cups and encourage the babies to replicate what you've done
- copy a simple rhythm on a tambour or drum – or just make their own sound with it
- put on a hat/necklace of giant toy beads.

It's important to encourage and give praise for trying, even if the effort was unsuccessful on this occasion, or if only a small part of the new skill was learned.

Comedy Turn

Focus	Group size	Preparation/Resources
Self-confidence and Self-esteem	Individual or small	Cushion Cuddly toy Clean, dry towel or flannel

Babies and toddlers like to be looked at and approved of. These ideas also appeal to babies' innate sense of fun and provide a gentle laugh for all.

- Have the baby create a 'joke' or piece of comedy by encouraging a copy of something you have just done that made her/him laugh. Once you have established that the baby has responded to the humour in any of the games, help her/him to recreate the humour, with you on the receiving end.
- First clap your hands together, then 'clap' them onto your own or the baby's cheeks at the end of each line of 'Pat-a-cake, Pat-a-cake, baker's MAN' (gently hold the baby's hands and clap them together, then separate the hands and guide them to clap softly onto the baby's own cheeks).
- Fall carefully but with a comedic 'Aaaargh!' onto a big cushion (gently help the baby to keel over onto the cushion and say 'Aaaargh').
- Make a mildly surprised, squeaky noise and pull a face every time [Teddy] appears from behind your shoulder (make [Teddy] appear suddenly from behind the baby's shoulder and elicit a surprised action or sound).
- Slowly pull a towel or hat down over your face, saying 'Goodbye' as you disappear, and 'Hello' as you whip it away (help the baby gently to pull a small towel or hat over her/his own face, and say 'Hello!' or 'Boo!').
- Have fun with innovating, taking your lead from the child.

Safety note

Not all babies are willing to have their faces covered, even briefly.

Non-breathable materials should never be placed over a baby's or child's face.

IDEA

17

Build a Nest

Focus	Group size	Preparation/Resources
All six aspects	Individual or small	Cosy corner with, e.g. picture books, cushions, blanket(s), cuddly toys CD or tape player with easy-listening music Breaktime drinks

Involving small children in designing and arranging their own cosy area helps them to gain confidence in their own ability to influence events. The snuggling time which follows this activity will be enjoyed as well.

- Depending on age and ability, either have the cushions, blankets, books and so on already on hand, or have them easily accessible but needing to be fetched by the children.
- Support children as they help to collect, pass or simply hold for a minute, the various 'cosy' accessories. Talk to your 'helpers' all the time, using their names and giving them elements of choice wherever possible, for example: '[Petra], which cushion shall we use to fill in this big gap?/Which of these books shall we read together?/Can we find a little table to put the drinks on?/Where can [Jamilah's] dolly sit to wait for her?'
- Invite each of the children during the operation, to 'test' the comfort, and to help make necessary adjustments before everyone snuggles in to appreciate the relaxing drinks, cuddle and book together.
- Play the music throughout, or just at snuggling time.
- Thank the children for their help in making it look so cosy, mentioning the touches that were added by individual children.

20

Hush-a-bye Toddler

Focus	Group size	Preparation/Resources
Dispositions and Attitudes	Individual	None
Self-confidence and Self-esteem		
Sense of Community		

The actions accompanying this traditional lullaby help to emphasize the comfort and security provided by the child's carer. The actions can be achieved either with the adult standing, or seated for a heavier child, with the child cradled just above the lap.

Say or sing gently:

Hush-a-bye [Daniel] on the treetop. (gently sway arms with the toddler cradled like a baby)
When the wind blows (puff out cheeks and blow gently)
The cradle will rock. (hold the child a little closer while making the 'cradle' judder as it continues to sway gently)
When the bough breaks, the cradle will fall . . . (hold the child more securely while suddenly 'dropping' arms a few inches to convey falling, saying 'CRASH!')
Down will come [Daniel], cradle and all. (end with a hug and say 'I've got you!')

I haven't met a toddler yet who hasn't enjoyed being cradled and rocked like a baby for this song.

IDEA

19

Little Helper

Focus	Group size	Preparation/Resources
Behaviour and Self-control Self-care	1 or 2	Items appropriate to whichever daily routine you choose to work with

This activity involves children in their own personal care, also helping them towards a simple understanding of how to select appropriate resources.

- Have necessary items easily accessible. Encourage a younger baby simply to pass to you, or an older child to fetch from nearby, the accessories for their own personal routines. These could be practical and comfort items for the mid-morning nap routine (nappy, box of baby wipes, cuddly toy or blanket, picture book) or a tin of food, bowl and spoon and cup/bottle for lunch.
- Praise and thank the baby for helping. As you use each item, talk about where the baby found it.

Taking this further

Progress to asking children to retrieve items from increasingly far-flung places.

Where's Your Teddy Gone?

Focus	Group size	Preparation/Resources
Dispositions and Attitudes Self-confidence and Self-esteem Making Relationships Behaviour and Self-control	1 or 2	The baby's favourite cuddly toy Pram quilt/blanket or a clean towel

This engages babies in a little role play, first helping to 'hide' a cuddly toy and then helping to 'find' it again, just for fun.

- Find a 'hiding' place, such as under a table, to put the cuddly toy, and then cover it with the quilt so that no bits stick out.
- Leave the room or area where the toy is, and then call out together '[Bear], where are you? We're coming to find you.'
- Spin out the notion for a minute that nobody knows where [Bear] is, then start 'searching', trying to divert the children from making a beeline for the hiding place.
- When the cuddly toy has been found, encourage a big fuss to be made of the toy, then play the game again if it's still enjoyable.

Pavlov's Baby

Focus	Group size	Preparation/Resources
Self-care	Individual or small	Simple ingredients to make the children's meals Gong (improvise using a tin tray or biscuit tin lid with wooden spoon beater) or a tinkly bell, musical toy or hooter

Letting young children become involved in the choice and preparation of a simple meal, even if only from a jar, will help them anticipate their food with pride and pleasure. The addition of the gong to the routine can add an extra incentive to sit down and eat.

• Let the children see you preparing their meal. If possible, allow them a small choice of menu, or which dish/spoon they would like to use. If they are able, encourage children to help with, for example, spooning the food out of the jar or transferring pieces of fruit from a plate into their own bowls.
• When the food is ready to eat, gently bang a gong to announce that it's time to eat at the table.
• When they are accustomed to the routine, let the children help with or take charge of banging the gong.

Safety note

Make sure that children see you washing your hands before preparing their food, and that they always wash theirs before they help in food preparation and before eating.

Baby Band

Focus	Group size	Preparation/Resources
Dispositions and Attitudes Self-confidence and Self-esteem Making Relationships	2–4, with adults to support	Wooden spoons for beaters Variety of beatable items, such as strong cardboard boxes, hollow plastic objects, shakers of all kinds or any baby-safe percussion instruments

This provides children with practice in turn-taking, as well as helping them to gain confidence and to receive approval.

- Having sat the children out of arm's reach of one another, give each child a shaker or a beater and something to beat. Let the children experiment with making sounds.
- Try to teach them to respond to the cue 'Stop', given with a smile and a purpose-made hand-signal.
- With the help of further adults to prompt individual children, try 'conducting' the children by calling their names individually and gesturing to them to play or stop or by kneeling in front of each one in turn, saying the child's name and miming the action of the instrument he or she is using.
- If they are at the upper end of the age range and are doing really well, aim to have them play sometimes individually, in pairs or all together. You may be able to convey the concept of waiting for a cue to have your turn, but expect this activity to sound a bit random.
- Before the musicians quite quickly feel the urge to get up and leave, bring over a child 'audience' to applaud the band's efforts.

Don't worry if, despite your attempts to structure it, the toddlers just make non-stop music until the instruments are put away. Equally, some of them may not feel up to making music at all that day.

Where's the Other One?

Focus	Group size	Preparation/Resources
Dispositions and Attitudes Self-confidence and Self-esteem	Individual or small	Make 6–8 cards/A5 sheets of paper, into 3–4 matching pairs. Draw circles, ladybirds, cars, the baby's initials in block letters or cut and paste pictures of toys from identical catalogues or from the internet Prepare pairs of other items such as matching cushions, pairs of bright gloves or socks, and play figures

This game involves children in looking closely at a picture or object and persevering with finding a match.

- Spread out one half of all the pairs on a table, sofa or the floor. Look at them with the child and discuss what's there.
- Give the child the other cards or objects one at a time and ask her/him to find the pair.
- Vary the way you phrase the questions, for example:
    - 'Have you got another one the same as this?'
    - 'Please can you find..?'
    - 'I need two, please.'

Taking this further

For an extra challenge, leave the child to find the pairs 'from cold', i.e. without discussing the objects first.

Spot the Difference

Focus	Group size	Preparation/Resources
Dispositions and Attitudes Sense of Community	Individual or small	Readily available props

This encourages young children to be interested in and to notice changes in their environment.

- Alter objects/details in the child's everyday environment. Suggestions include:
    - Placing a bath duck in the child's cot.
    - Swapping round a piece of puzzle from two favourite puzzles.
    - Putting mismatching shoes on the child.
    - Dressing a favourite cuddly toy in a glove.
    - Breaking any normally unchanging routine, such as using a different spoon at meal time, or a different coloured flannel or towel at bath time.
- See if the child notices anything different without being prompted, but otherwise draw attention to the 'odd' detail in a surprised and interested tone of voice. When she/he spots the difference, chat about what's going on, for example: 'Oh dear, we've got a red shoe and a brown shoe here! That's not right, is it? We need two shoes the same. Which shoes do you want to wear today, red or brown? Please can you go and get the other brown one, then?'
- The child can help to put everything back to 'normal' after the game.

Having a Good Sort Out

Focus	Group size	Preparation/Resources
Dispositions and Attitudes Self-confidence and Self-esteem	Individual or small	4 medium boxes, e.g. toy boxes/ adults' shoe boxes Plenty of components for different sets of things, e.g. plastic bricks, wooden spoons, toy cars, clean socks

- Let the children see you sorting out a pile of mixed items into the four boxes. Commentate on your actions: 'Bricks in the blue box, spoons in the green box, socks in the black box . . .'
- Invite the children to help you finish the task, providing a similar running commentary on their progress.
- Thank the helpers and let them help you put the boxes somewhere satisfyingly neat, where you can keep them and be seen to use them for a while.

Greetings, My Friend

Focus	Group size	Preparation/Resources
Sense of Community	Any	1 blank, folded card per child Range of art materials to decorate cards, e.g. cut-out shapes, sponge shapes or picture stamps to print Ready-mixed paint

Making and giving a card to a significant person in their family or playgroup can help children see themselves as an important member of that group. Children may choose who they want to give their card to, for example, their dad/sister/nan/favourite cuddly toy/pet. If the cards are to be given to family members for recognized celebrations, such as Mothers' Day or Id-ul-Fitr, even small children will enjoy participating in the celebrations and customs of their families.

- Although children of this age need much support with sticking, printing or stamping the design onto the first side of the card, resist the impulse to help too much, so that their gift will be all their own work.
- Help them to draw or over-write a kiss, smiley face or their initial. Talk to the children about who the card is for, so that they think about the special person as they work. If they are unsure, help them decide who the recipient could be.
- If preparing the cards for Mothers' Day, remember to make provision for any of the children whose mother is not around for any reason to give the card to a different, special female relative or carer.
- If Muslim children or others make a card to celebrate, for example, the Festival of Id-ul-Fitr, the card should be designed with the fold on the right-hand side, to be read from right to left.

SECTION 3

16 – 26 months

Toddlers at this stage are becoming more assertive, sometimes possessive, and often attention seeking. They may interact confidently with adults and enjoy being the centre of attention and gaining approval. They ask questions – plenty – and often chat happily to friendly adults, even unfamiliar ones.

Toddlers want to see and know everything, soaking up new experiences and vocabulary like a sponge. A two year old may have around 100 words in her or his repertoire, and can communicate by forming them into short, two- or three-word sentences. By the end of this stage children start to understand the significance of 'in a minute' and 'soon', even though they might dislike being expected to wait.

IDEA 27

Don't Wake the Baby

Focus	Group size	Preparation/Resources
Making Relationships Sense of Community	Any	Baby doll or cuddly toy, wrapped in a blanket

Appealing to the caring side of their natures, this idea helps small children to realize that babies have particular needs. It also provides an opportunity to remind them that they were also beautiful babies once, and enjoyed all the special 'perks'.

- The children sit closely together in a circle. Explain that the doll is tired, but would like to see everyone before she has a sleep. Tell them that small babies sleep *a lot*.
- Pass the doll, wrapped in the blanket, around the circle. Encourage the children not to shout but to speak quietly and pass smoothly and carefully. Give a kindly reminder if the baby is knocked or dropped. As the last few children receive the baby, ask everyone to whisper now, as the baby has gone to sleep because she feels safe and everyone has been so gentle and quiet.
- Put the baby to bed in another room, and ask the children to remain fairly quiet for a short time while the baby has a nap.

Taking this further

Talk with the children about how they were babies too and how everybody kept as quiet as possible so they could sleep. Invite parents to come in and show or lend their child's baby photos. These can be admired, and will help to confirm that each of them was a sweet baby who had a turn at being cosseted too.

Bang! Sssh!

Focus	Group size	Preparation/Resources
Making Relationships Behaviour and Self-control Sense of Community	Any	Cuddly toy or doll 'friend'

Children need to be made aware of the needs of others – in this case, a toy friend who is 'ill'– and to realize that their actions affect others.

- Explain that the 'friend', let's say Teddy, is not feeling very well today and may need to lie down. Talk with the children to guess what might be wrong with Teddy. Some of them may recall their own recent colds or bouts of sickness to help them relate to a sick person's need to have peace and quiet.
- The children stand in a space facing you. When Teddy is held up in the air, looking bright and well, the children are allowed to stamp and clap, saying 'Bang, Bang!' They need to keep their eye on Teddy, though, because when he lies down (cradled in your arms), the children must walk around quietly, with a finger against their lips until he gets up again.
- Prompt the children if necessary by saying, 'Poor Teddy wants to lie down now. Sssh.' or 'Oh, good, he's better now, you can carry on!'

Safety note

If the children are moving around for this game in a fairly large room, encourage them always to walk into an empty space to avoid collisions.

Gourmet Snacks

Focus	Group size	Preparation/Resources
Dispositions and Attitudes Self-confidence and Self-esteem Making Relationships Self-care Sense of Community	Any	5 different, ready-prepared healthy foods for snacks (e.g. a variety of washed, sliced/ segmented fruit; raisins), perhaps with variations from the kind of snack the children normally have in their nursery setting Sets of small, clean plastic containers to hold the different foods Children's individual bowls or plates

An early interest in healthy food, along with any food hygiene routines taught carefully at this age, will stay with the children for life. For this activity, children choose from a small selection of healthy foods, and help present the food tastefully for their own snack.

- Put the ingredients for the children's snacks into the containers, one variety per container, such as apple slices in one, banana halves in another, raisins in another. Prepare enough complete sets of food (five containers, each with different food) for each group of four children to have their own set.
- Make sure all the children wash their hands thoroughly and dry them on paper or clean towels just before sitting down to the table.
- Bring a group of four to the table. Help the children select three to five items for their snack, and arrange them on their individual plates however they like. You may have demonstrated some ideas beforehand – for example, all items grouped in the centre or around the outside of the plate. A small handful of raisins counts as one item.
- Aim to have the children sit and wait for everyone in their group to be ready before they start eating together.

Safety note

Particularly as children may be trying out food that's new to them, watch out for choking.

Taking this further

Provide folded serviettes/kitchen-roll squares.

Make a point of recycling any waste food from this activity – send it home for rabbits/birds/compost as appropriate.

IDEA 30

Is that a New Hat?

Focus	Group size	Preparation/Resources
Sense of Community	Any	(See below)

This focuses on children's powers of observation, helping them to take an interest in their environment and to notice details.

- Adults change a part of their appearance or add/remove things from the normal environment for, let's say, the last half hour of the morning session. Don't prime the children at all. Appoint an adult observer to see if the children seem to notice any changes. They may do a double-take, laugh to themselves, point or stare, but may not actually say anything.
- Here are a few suggestions for 'noticeable' changes that can easily be made, but have fun devising your own:
  - Wear extremely unmatched shoes or only one shoe, and hobble if no one has noticed.
  - Put on a funny hat.
  - Tie a brightly coloured scarf somewhere, such as on the playhouse door frame.
  - Stand a few dolls/cuddly toys on their heads on a bookcase or windowsill.
  - Introduce two or three new bowls/plates for snack time or offer a different fruit variety, e.g. rosy apples if they're accustomed to green.
  - Pin bright pairs of gloves or a packet of crisps randomly onto a noticeboard or wall display.
- At the end of the session, perhaps in circle time, the 'observer' praises individual children who have been using their eyes, and who spotted, without prompting, anything unusual during the session.
- If any particular changes went unnoticed, give clues such as, 'Can you see anything on the [playhouse] that wasn't there before?' 'Is [helper] wearing anything funny today?' Go on to make sure that the children have spotted or at least have been shown all the changes.
- Incorporate questions into the daily routine which extend the children's observational skills. For example, tell them that today there'll be a piece of equipment they haven't seen before and they can tell a helper when they think they've spotted it.

New Achievements

Focus	Group size	Preparation/Resources
Dispositions and Attitudes	Individual or	2–3 floor cushions
Self-confidence and	small	Plastic bowl, cup and spoon
Self-esteem		Ingredients to make a sandwich
Self-care		Painting materials and aprons
		Access to a PC (optional)

This is essentially a list of achievable, fun skills which give the children opportunities to succeed and to grow in self-confidence.

Teach the children to:

- put two or three cushions squarely on top of one another and sit proudly on top of the pile
- spoon fresh water out of a clean bowl into a clean cup, and drink it (with or without spouted lid. Children may need help replacing tight lids)
- draw or overdraw a smiley face
- make a yeast extract/honey sandwich
- paint inside a drawn circle to make a sun/ball/flower centre
- bring up a prepared picture on the computer by left-clicking on the mouse to maximize it
- walk backwards carefully, holding on to a helper's hands.

Encourage the children to show off their new skills, where appropriate without any help.

Weather the Weather

Focus	Group size	Preparation/Resources
Self-care	Any	None

Small children often have definite ideas about which clothes they do and don't want to wear. This activity helps them think about what they actually need to wear to match the weather.

- Ask parents if, just for today, they would mind not removing any outdoor garments their children are wearing when they arrive.
- If possible, look out of the window with the children to decide what sort of weather we have today, or stand outside briefly in a safe place together. Point out clues as to the weather, for example:
    - Rainy weather: puddles/car windscreen wipers/rain running down windows/umbrellas.
    - Sunny: blue sky/white clouds/shadows/people wearing sunglasses.
    - Windy: leaves or litter blowing about/clothes flapping/howling sounds/the children's hats being blown off.
    - Snowy or icy: footprints and scrunchy sounds underfoot/cold hands and ears/swirling snow/plants covered with snow/slippery paths.
- Come back in to discuss the children's ideas, as they sit in their [coats], about today's weather, then decide together which clothes are best for today and why, e.g. 'Brrr! It's cold outside, but [Esther] is wearing a lovely big coat to keep her warm,' or 'Phew! That sun is really hot today. I see some of you have brought a sun hat/sun cream so you can play in the sandpit outside.'
- Be diplomatic if any children have arrived without sensible clothing.
- Confirm that we don't need coats indoors and help the children to hang up their coats ready for the next time they go outside.

Taking this further

With slightly older children, explore the different benefits/uses of rain, such as puddles and fun/watering the plants/filling up duck ponds/washing the streets.

Foster a respect for rain, because we need it.

Glad Rags

Focus	Group size	Preparation/Resources
Self-confidence and Self-esteem Self-care	Small	Full-length safety mirror Simple dressing-up clothes with easy or no fastenings, for as much independence as possible

From a fairly early age, children can be encouraged to show preferences about which clothes they feel 'good' in.

- Help children to dress in clothes of their choice, then point out positive results in the mirror, e.g. 'That jacket is the same colour as your hair', or 'You look very smart in those shoes', or 'That handbag looks lovely with those pretty shoes.'
- Although not all children choose to play at dressing up, they often enjoy being admired, and this session should be kept quite low key. Encourage the children to look at their reflection and to tweak/smooth/fluff up the clothes and add accessories, and to take pride in how they look.
- Try and elicit some feedback from each child as to what, specifically, they like about their reflection. Children in response, may say such things as 'my hair' or even 'you' if you are in the frame too, but may also make it clear they have fallen in love with the shoes, handbag or Spiderman top.

Safety note
Avoid draping hem lines/hats that cover the eyes and take care with anything that may be put around the neck.

Taking this further
If the children are having fun and you feel they are confident enough, stage a mini-parade with a little background nursery music as they walk through the main space.

Pet Subjects

Focus	Group size	Preparation/Resources
Sense of Community	Any	Ask parents to lend photographs of family members or pets who are special to the children. Photos should be clearly labelled by the family, with the names of the child/relatives/pets plus any interesting facts or anecdotes about them. If it's difficult to organize photos from families, use either a book with clear illustrations of different pets, or photos of your own pets.

Discussing either family members or pets at home reinforces the child's sense of her/himself as a member of a family.

• Have the owner of the photo sit or stand with you, facing the other children; help them to hold up the photo for the others to see.
• Find out little snippets of information from the child, basing your questions on the information provided on the back of the photo by the family, for example: 'Shall we ask [Lorenzo] what his baby sister's name is?' '[Anna] – that's a lovely name.' '[Jamie] has got a sister called [Anna], haven't you, [Jamie]?' Or: '[Janine's] dog did something silly. [Janine], did your dog eat something off the kitchen table? Was he sick somewhere? Where? What did your mummy say? [Luke], I think *your* dog did something silly yesterday, didn't he?'
• Ask for hands up who has: a sister/the same pet as the one being discussed/ a similar story to tell; hands up who likes [Janine's] dog.
• List aloud the names of the children who all have a sister/who like [Janine's] dog, and so on, to make all the children feel they belong to the group. Make a point of drawing in any children who haven't been included – they could be the group who are the only child in their family or who don't have any pets or who like cats but not dogs.

The Stain Test

Focus	Group size	Preparation/Resources
Self-care	Small	Various clean towelling fabric bibs or different coloured flannels, plus some bibs or flannels with 'artificial dirt'– try diluted green food colouring or smeared chocolate A bowl or bucket of warm water with a little 'sensitive' grade soap, soap liquid or powder 2–3 buckets of clean water for rinses Waterproof protection for the children's clothes and the floor

This introduces the notion of 'clean' and 'dirty' and the need for soap and water for washing.

- Show a nice clean bib next to a dirty one, having a similar pair ready for each child. Pick up your clean bib, showing how lovely and clean and soft it is, rubbing it next to your cheek and saying, 'M-mmm, that's all clean,' looking pleased. Then with a frown, pick up the dirty one, saying, 'Ugh! That's dirty. That needs a WASH!' The children repeat 'clean', 'dirty' and 'wash'.
- Help the children to decide which of their own pair of bibs is clean and which is dirty, encouraging them to use some of the appropriate vocabulary: 'dirty', 'wash', 'clean'.
- Help each of the children in turn to give their dirty bib a good swish about and a rub in the suds, then a squeeze and at least two rinses, changing the rinse water as necessary. Use the words 'dripping', 'squeeze', 'rinse' and 'wet'.
- See if the children spot the coloured 'dirty' water.
- Blot the clean, wet bibs on clean towels and guide children to understand that now the 'dirt' has gone, they have two clean bibs.
- Let the children help to empty the used water down the plughole. Dry the bibs on a radiator or peg them up to dry.
- Make sure the children thoroughly wash, rinse and dry their hands to finish.

Taking this further
If you prefer, demonstrate the washing of a genuinely dirty item, letting the children watch at a dry distance.

Safety note
Ensure that the floor remains slip-proof throughout.

IDEA
36

Missing Piece

Focus	Group size	Preparation/Resources
Dispositions and Attitudes Behaviour and Self-control Self-care	Individual	Wooden inset puzzle or shape-posting activity

When given opportunities to be assertive in non-threatening situations, children can learn strategies to stand up for themselves in future. This activity also aims to develop children's confidence to persevere with a chosen task.

- Let the child choose a wooden inset puzzle or post-it game, then give support while it's being played with.
- Briefly hold back or part-cover the last piece, so that the child has to tell you it's not there.
- Praise the child for telling you and reveal the missing piece. Clap or cheer when the puzzle is completed. Tell other adults/older children how sensible the child was.
- Bring attention to and praise any incidental acts of assertiveness in the course of a day, contrasting these with unacceptably over-assertive behaviour.

 Taking this further

Further ideas to encourage children to pipe up confidently:

- Leave a key accessory out of the dressing-up box, e.g. one shoe from a pair, or the helmet from the fireman's set.
- Say 'Put your coats on' when you really mean 'Take them off'.
- Momentarily forget to give a paintbrush or play dough to two children in a group at the craft table.
- Call the snack 'orange' as you distribute it, when it is in fact apple.
- Use the wrong name for a character throughout a familiar story, until someone stops you.

IDEA

37

Feed the Birds

Focus	Group size	Preparation/Resources
Behaviour and Self-control Self-care	Any (usual adult to child ratio for outings)	Strong paper bags/plastic or card boxes Freshly chopped soft grass Lettuce leaves Hand wipes

While feeding the swans and ducks in the park, children learn to be aware of the needs of living things. This activity also reinforces the need for hand hygiene.

- The children decide, from a limited range, which containers/bags (plastic food boxes/paper bags/card containers) are best to hold the food for the birds.
- Explain to the children that although lots of people give bread to the birds, fresh, green food is actually better for ducks and swans. The children help to fill their own bags or boxes with the grass and/or lettuce.
- Once at the park or gardens, ensure that all children have a fair turn at feeding the birds before they feel full up and lose interest. Keep an eye on children who are afraid of birds, especially if the birds come over to your group in large numbers.
- Praise the children for not chasing the birds.
- Make a point of recycling the used containers if possible, along with any leftover food.
- When you are ready to leave the feeding area, use the hand wipes to freshen hands temporarily.

Safety note
Remind the children not to touch their mouths or faces until they have washed their hands back at base.

Garden World

Focus	Group size	Preparation/Resources
Dispositions and Attitudes Self-confidence and Self-esteem	1–2 children per adult	Parent helpers Seasonal vegetables/fruit (shop-bought or harvested) Appropriate permission (e.g. allotment association) and a pre-visit to the plot

Visiting local private gardens or allotments provides children with an opportunity to explore their natural environment.

- Before making your way to the garden vegetable plot or allotment, let the children handle and name samples of some of the fruit and vegetables they might see growing. Ask if they have seen or eaten any of them before.
- Depending on the time of year, on the way to the allotment/vegetable plot draw attention to:
  - bugs and worms
  - falling and fallen leaves
  - snails
  - fungi (with warnings)
  - signs of wildlife, such as birds' nests, rabbit pellets and lawns dug up by badgers looking for worms (have pictures of the creatures involved to show before or after the nature walk)
  - birds and bird calls or songs
  - berries that are safe for the birds but not for us to eat
  - contrast between areas of grass that have/have not been cut
  - gardeners digging/watering, using watering cans/rain butts/hoses
  - huts and sheds (what do the children think may be inside?).
- Ask your allotment 'host' if the children may peep inside the shed, also if they could see how carrots are pulled or potatoes dug up, and watch the cutting or picking of a few 'surface' fruits or vegetables. Easily identifiable things that the children can see growing include most fruits, bean varieties, courgettes, cabbages, sprouts, cauliflowers, leeks and onions, tomatoes and cucumbers.

Safety note

Although the children should be encouraged to 'touch and feel' at the allotment when invited, apply all normal hygiene routines.

A Sort of Assault Course

Focus	Group size	Preparation/Resources
Making Relationships Behaviour and Self-control	2–6	Set up an 'assault course' with simple objects, such as a large cushion, kitchen-roll tubes taped together, a strong, shallow box with rope attached for pulling, a play tunnel or sheet/material to drape over chairs to create a tunnel, a wheeled sit-on toy

As well as being fun, this game gives practice in waiting, sharing and turn-taking, and in keeping to simple boundaries and rules.

- Having set up the assault course, demonstrate what each child will do in a specified order, for example (using the resources suggested above): 'Run to the cushion and curl up on it like a cat. Jump over the kitchen-roll tubes. Sit in the box and [an adult] pulls you to the tunnel. Climb through the tunnel. Sit on the toy car and ride to [another adult] at the finish.'
- Emphasize the rules regarding the completion of the course, and waiting and turn-taking.
- Encourage all children involved to clap each competitor. An adult could announce why each child's attempt was special.

A Pat on the Back

Focus	Group size	Preparation/Resources
Behaviour and Self-control	Any	Optional reward scheme, e.g. chart with individuals' names and smiley-face stickers

In order to foster the children's personal, social and emotional development, carers need consistently to reinforce positive behaviour. Use every practical opportunity to draw attention to and praise a child or group of children who have shown that:

- they are responding to a simple boundary or expectation, such as asking to have a toy out from a cupboard instead of helping themselves, or giving up a ride-on toy to another child even though they may still be enjoying their turn
- they are aware of the consequences of their actions or words, such as kindly letting another child into the playhouse or saying thank you to other children or adults
- they are showing care for others, living things or their environment, such as helping up or showing concern for a child who has fallen over/wanting to feed the birds/telling an adult about a spillage.

Talk about the possible consequences of, for example, *not* telling an adult that they've dropped their drink. During circle time draw attention to any special behaviour and say why it is good. Children love hearing kind words about themselves, and being admired may be enough reward. However, a fair and consistent reward system can be a powerful tool and you may feel that a formal reward is appropriate when the children in your care show particularly special qualities that you'd like the others to emulate. Suggestions include:

- A simple 'pat on the back' (children can reach back and give themselves a little pat on the shoulder).
- A wall chart with children's names and reward stickers.
- An interactive wall display with, for example, sugar-paper 'feathers' with the children's names on inserted into a cardboard hat with slits, or smiley-face 'suns' as flower centres decorated by the children.
- A small privilege such as helping to give out the fruit snack to their group.
- A personalized note to inform a parent or carer of the lovely piece of behaviour.

Up a Bit, Right a Bit

Focus	Group size	Preparation/Resources
Dispositions and Attitudes	4+	Art materials to make, e.g. cats/fish/stars/circles/ faces
Self-confidence and Self-esteem		Display space at child level, such as a plain wall with boundaries of the display marked out, or a couple of painting easels side by side
Making Relationships		Lots of Blu-Tack

For this idea, the children are given a free rein with where to place their designs on a designated area, creating a display that is almost entirely their own work.

- Cut out the children's designs ready for display. Blu-Tack the back of each one.
- Decide whether it's best for the children to go up to the display singly, in pairs or in larger groups.
- As their turn arrives, give each child their own Blu-Tacked design. Children choose independently where they'd like to place their design, although some need help to make the design stay up there.
- At story/circle time encourage individuals to come up and point to their best bit, generally showing your own interest in the children's display.

Yours or Mine?

Focus	Group size	Preparation/Resources
Behaviour and Self-control Sense of Community	3+	Verbal or written agreement from parents/carers to send in a child-safe, non-precious toy from home Box to hold all the toys brought by the children Name tag or removable label to attach to every toy brought by the children Second box full of toys to share Two big, different coloured signs to label the boxes: 'Please take only your own toy' and 'Toys for everyone'

This addresses the need for children to understand about other people's belongings.

- Point out that the [red] label tells you that the toys inside that box belong to the person whose name is on the toy label, so we must only take the toy with our own name on it.
- Explain that the toys in the box with the [green] sign are for everybody to share, and should be returned afterwards ready for another little girl or boy to use.
- Help particularly with the comings and goings of the children's own, labelled toys, encouraging children to take only one toy at a time to play with.
- When all the toys are tidied away, congratulate the children on being careful with them and on making sure that the toys have all ended up safe and in the right places.

 Safety note
While labelling the toys with the children's names as they arrive, you will be able to 'vet' them for safety.

22 – 36 months

This stage is particularly significant in the development of self-esteem. Although still needing comfort and praise from key people, children are also rapidly gaining a sense of their own identity, which can create conflict between the emerging independent spirit and the need to be approved of. They need to be reassured that although adults may disapprove of their behaviour, they themselves are loved the same as ever.

Children begin to make friends, just starting to play cooperatively with, rather than alongside, them. By the end of this stage, waiting, turn-taking and sharing may be easier to encourage, although may not come unsolicited until later.

War on Germs

Focus	Group size	Preparation/Resources
Self-care	Any	Toothbrush, toothpaste and tumbler to mime toothbrush routine Soap, bowl of water and towel Pictures of dirty and/or clean teeth (optional)

Through simple songs, children are reminded how to take care of their personal hygiene.

Dental hygiene
- Talk about the way bits of food can stay in your mouth and go bad, and that's why we need to clean our teeth and gums and rinse all the bits away.
- Talk about looking after your teeth to keep them strong, and how your mouth smells nice when you've got clean teeth.
- Ask who knows how to clean their teeth/when do we clean our teeth/who likes the taste of toothpaste in their mouth/what colour toothbrush do they like best?
- Talk through and mime the tooth-brushing routine, reminding the children that we spit out, not swallow. To mime 'spitting', bow your head and blow the 'water' out.
- Teach the teeth-cleaning song, with mime: (to the tune of 'Row, row, row your boat')
  Brush, brush, brush your teeth,
  Gently – and your gums. (keeping the tune going, mime sipping water, then with lips closed pretend to swill the water about in your mouth)
  Mmm mmm,
  Mmm mmm,
  Mmm mmm , mmm mmm, mmmmm – Whoooph! (mime spitting)

Hand hygiene
- Introduce simply the concept of dirt and germs. Demonstrate or mime nearly picking up a piece of apple to eat, but realizing you haven't washed your hands yet. You could emphasize the point by touching the floor or something grubby before the apple.
- Tell the children you are going to wash your hands so that the germs don't go on the apple, into your mouth and your tummy and make you ill.
- Demonstrate washing and drying your hands. Talk about the germs in the water and being able to throw them away down the plughole with the water.
- Show your nice clean hands, then pick up and eat the apple slice.
- Teach the hand-washing song: (the tune of 'Row, row, row your boat' is re-used here, to link together the two aspects of personal hygiene in the children's minds.)
  Wash, wash, wash your hands,
  Time for dinner now.
  Rub-a-dub, rub-a-dub,
  Dry them on the towel.

Rabbit Blues

Focus	Group size	Preparation/Resources
Dispositions and Attitudes	Any	Cuddly toy or hand-puppet rabbit, or
Making Relationships		similarly appealing/familiar character
Behaviour and Self-control		Carrot (optional)
Sense of Community		

Children are encouraged to think of ways to help cheer up Rabbit.

- Tell the group that poor Rabbit is sad today. Animate the toy to show he is off colour, e.g. shaking his head when asked if he wants to play or eat a carrot. The children may be able to think of possible reasons for his sadness, relating their ideas to things that have made them unhappy themselves.
- Find out what makes the children feel happy generally. Ask how they think Rabbit could be cheered up. Typical ideas include: giving him a cuddle; taking him swimming/shopping/to the seaside/to see his mummy; buying him sweets. If children recommend a cuddle, holding his hand or any other immediately available remedy, encourage them to try it, with a noticeable improvement in Rabbit's demeanour.
- Thank the children for their ideas and show them that Rabbit is feeling much better just hearing about all those lovely kind things.

Take it Away

Focus	Group size	Preparation/Resources
Dispositions and Attitudes	Small, medium or 1 to 1	Emotive items such as a toy spider, a snake, Brussels sprouts, a doll, a football Clean, lidded box, with a big sign saying 'FAR AWAY', and an oversized mock postage stamp

Children are encouraged to express their opinions and preferences about a range of creatures, foods and activities.

- Hold up one of the items, say the toy snake, and invite the children to comment. Who likes the snake? What do each of them like about it? Who doesn't like it and how does it make them feel? Ensure that the children listen to one another.
- Ask the children what they want to do with the snake, aiming for a democratic (hands up) decision whether to keep it or put it in the box and send it far away.
- Repeat with other items/activities the children may have opinions on, such as having a bath or going shopping – represented by a bath duck/purse respectively.
- At the end of the session, tape up the box with the rejected items and promise the children that you will send it 'far away'.

Compliments to the Chef

Focus	Group size	Preparation/Resources
Making Relationonships Self-care	3–5	Up-to-date records of dietary needs, including allergies, of all the children taking part Simple, child-safe kitchen utensils for food preparation Disposable plates/cutlery for the 'diners' Ingredients for a simple, savoury recipe, e.g. if basic cooking facilities are available, warmed spaghetti or baked beans with grated cheese; toast and marmite/smooth peanut butter If there are no cooking facilities, try ready-cooked cold pasta with a jar of dressing, or triangle or round (pastry cutter) sandwiches

Becoming a chef for a while gives little ones a chance to follow rules, to take pride in their finished product, and to be thanked and appreciated . . .
. . . and becoming diners helps children to communicate their likes and dislikes, while thinking of the needs of others.

- Select one group as the chefs and another, the same size, as the diners.
- Make sure all hands are washed and dried.
- Establish simple food hygiene rules during preparation.
- All the chefs prepare the same savoury recipe and serve their dish to the diners.
- Ask the diners if they like their meals and help them to find something positive to say, even if it's only 'Thank you'.
- Encourage all participants to help with clearing away.
- Aim for the children to reverse roles on another occasion.

Raising the Bar

Focus	Group size	Preparation/Resources
Dispositions and Attitudes Self-confidence and Self-esteem Making Relationships	Any	Long skipping rope

As well as giving practice in waiting and turn-taking, these two skipping rope games give children a chance to try something a little bit different and daring.

Game one: Higher and higher
- Two adults each hold one end of the rope, standing apart so that the middle of the rope lies along the ground for at least two metres. A third adult stands with the children lined up at right angles to and facing the rope, and two or three metres away from it.
- The children run forward one at a time and jump over the rope as it lies on the ground. When all have had a turn and are queuing on the other side of the rope with a fourth adult if available, the rope-holders lift the rope a few centimetres and the children again jump over one by one, finishing back where they first started. Repeat, raising the height only 2–3cm at a time.

Game two: Snakes
- The adults holding the rope crouch down and lay the rope on the ground along most of its length, then gently wiggle the rope on the ground. Each child in turn jumps over the 'snake' thus created. Expect a lot of squealing, as the snake can seem quite real.
- The wiggling can be slowed almost to a standstill for any children who need encouragement. If you prefer, give the snake a friendly name, refer to the rope as a worm or pretend the rope is a wave they have to jump over.

Safety note

Ensure that the children are jumping on a safe surface.

If any child looks as if they are running through the rope rather than jumping over it, the adults holding the rope should let it go immediately to avoid tripping.

Here Comes Teddy

Focus	Group size	Preparation/Resources
Dispositions and Attitudes Self-confidence and Self-esteem Making Relationships	5–6+	Small- to medium-sized cuddly toy for each group of 5–6

As well as being fun, team games help to develop cooperation.

- Children line up as straight as possible in groups, facing forward, an arm's length away from the child in front. Adult helpers try to prevent the teams drifting together if there's more than one team.
- The cuddly toy is passed from the front of each line to the back, each child passing him over their own head without turning round.
- When the last child in the line receives the toy, she or he runs forward and stands at the front of their line, passing the toy overhead to the second child, and so on until the team is back to (more or less) their original order.
- The whole team sits down to show completion.

Taking this further

If the children are able to maintain a reasonably straight tunnel standing with their legs apart, the cuddly toy can be passed or slid through the tunnel.

Use the cuddly toy as a 'baton' for a simple to and fro relay race.

My Favourite Things

Focus	Group size	Preparation/Resources
Dispositions and Attitudes	Small to	A cuddly toy
Self-confidence and Self-esteem	medium	
Making Relationships		
Self-care		
Sense of Community		

Children are encouraged to chat about themselves, and to take turns with speaking and listening. A cuddly toy passed on to the speaker each time indicates to the others that it is their turn to listen.

- Holding the cuddly toy, you say, 'I really like . . . [walking in the park].'
- Add some detail: 'I like [walking in the park so I can feed the ducks, and I don't mind if it's raining].'
- Pass the cuddly toy to the first child, who says, 'I really like . . . [jumping in puddles/fish fingers/my Nanny's house].' If no further information is forthcoming, prompt with a question.
- Pose a question to elicit at least a 'Yes' or 'No' answer from any child unwilling to speak, and welcome any contribution.
- Use different openers such as, 'I'm good at . . .'/'I wish . . .'

Now You See It . . .

Focus	Group size	Preparation/Resources
Dispositions and Attitudes	Any	Tray or table set up with objects
Self-confidence and Self-esteem		within the children's experience
Making Relationships		Piece of light material to cover all
Sense of Community		the objects

The classic Kim's Game sharpens memory and concentration skills, building self-confidence as skills improve.

- Depending on the ages and abilities of the children, spread out three to six familiar objects on the tray and talk about each object to focus children's attention on memorable details, for example, 'This is a green tractor. Look, Freddie, it's the same colour as your shoes.'
- Cover all the objects with the piece of material, and without the children seeing, remove one of the objects.
- Remove the cover and see if the children can spot what's missing. If not, give clues based on the details you drew attention to, such as, 'There was something the same colour as Freddie's shoes but now it's gone.'
- Replace the missing object and repeat, removing either a different object each time, or one that's already had a turn at going missing.

Cheeky Chimp

Focus	Group size	Preparation/Resources
Making Relationships Behaviour and Self-control	Any	Chimp puppet or toy

Cheeky Chimp helps children to think about the difference between right and wrong.

- Tell children Chimp has just told you that, for a joke, he is going to throw water all over the children's coats/eat all the apples ready on plates for their snacks/stamp mud all over the floor from the garden.
- Find out the children's various thoughts on the matter. Some may think it would be funny or clever if he played those tricks. Ask children how they would feel if they had to put on a wet coat/miss their snack/clean up the mud.
- Discuss why it would be wrong of Chimp to do those things – because he would be spoiling other people's belongings/taking things that are not his/ making extra work for someone else.
- Ask Chimp if he has changed his mind about doing those things.
- Ask the children to think what they would say to Chimp if he did carry out the 'joke'.

IDEA

52

From The Roof Tops

Focus	Group size	Preparation/Resources
Self-confidence and Self-esteem Self-care	Small to medium	Make a 'megaphone' out of a semi-circle of card or sugar paper

This activity celebrates the children's positive qualities and achievements, building self-esteem.

- Children take turns to use the megaphone to announce what they are good at, such as writing the number 2, giving cuddles, washing up. Prompt where necessary.
- Encourage everyone to clap each achievement.

Taking this further

For older children, make a 'microphone' from a kitchen-roll tube covered in black or silver 'duck' (duct) tape, and 'interview' them about their success stories.

Working Together

Focus	Group size	Preparation/Resources
Dispositions and Attitudes	2+	Readily available items – see below.

Children become teachers and learners for this game. Split the group into two halves. If necessary, an adult can pair with a child to even up numbers.

- One half of the group is taken off for a story or circle time.
- Meanwhile, teach the rest of the group a new but simple skill, such as modelling with play dough, turning two snakes into linked circles/ assembling a card from cut-out shapes and drawing or overdrawing a kiss inside/doing the hand signs for 'I – love – you'.
- When the 'other halves' return, the children teach them, in pairs, how to achieve the new skill. Give plenty of support and praise for both teachers and learners.

IDEA

54

It's a Gift

Focus	Group size	Preparation/Resources
All six aspects	Any	Salt dough Art materials

All the children make a gift from salt dough for a special family member. Making the gifts can be an opportunity for everyone to learn about different families' traditions and celebrations.

- Help children to decide what they wish to make, and then to shape and style their model out of the salt dough. Help them to add their own details, e.g. roughing up the surface or adding eyes with a pencil tip.
- Make a note of who each child wants the recipient to be.
- Air dry or slow-cook the models. When completely cooled down, they can either be left plain or the children can paint them.
- Coat models with glue thinned with a little water.
- Encourage children to talk about their family customs with regard to celebrations and the giving and receiving of gifts.

Taking this further

Sponge-print, paint or roll designs onto paper to make gift-wrap.

The Bells!

Focus	Group size	Preparation/Resources
Dispositions and Attitudes Sense of Community	Small to medium	Simple percussion instruments such as sleigh bells and a tambour

This activity builds confidence in speaking in a familiar group and gives practice in turn-taking.

- Sitting in a circle, the children take turns to say, 'My name is [own name]', then shake the bells to match the rhythm of their name, for example: 'My name is Kath-ryn' – shake-shake or 'My name is Ben-ja-min'– shake-shake-shake.
- The other children in the circle 'echo' the percussion by clapping the same rhythm.
- The bells are passed on to the next child to say her or his own name and the process is repeated round the circle until everyone has had a turn.
- On a different day, a different instrument and a new sentence may be introduced, such as 'My favourite meal is . . .' [beans-on-toast – tap-tap-tap], with the other children in the circle either clapping as before or taking turns with a number of percussion instruments to 'echo' the rhythm.

IDEA

56

Perfect Trust

Focus	Group size	Preparation/Resources
Making Relationships Behaviour and Self-control	An even number, to play in pairs	1 ball per pair of children

This collaborative game helps to develop a sense of partnership and responsibility towards others.

- Children sit on the floor facing a partner, legs outstretched and feet wide apart. Feet rest on partners' feet, sole to sole, forming a diamond shape.
- Children gently roll the ball to each other within the diamond shape. They need to keep their four feet together so that the ball stays in play. If the ball escapes, encourage them to take turns to fetch it back.

Taking this further

One child makes a bridge with her/his legs while another pushes a free-wheeling toy car under the bridge. The car is caught by a third child on the other side and sent smoothly back. The 'bridges' must be able to trust that nothing dangerous is going to happen between their feet.

Hunt the Hearts

Focus	Group size	Preparation/Resources
Self-confidence and Self-esteem Making Relationships	Small to medium	Make red hearts from card – the same number of hearts as there are individual children, or pairs of children if working collaboratively. Hearts should be 8–15cm high, depending on age/abilities of children

This game gives practice either at persevering independently or working collaboratively in pairs.

- Show the children the hearts that you will be hiding.
- Either the children go out of the room, or the adult hiding the hearts goes into a different room. The hearts are hidden leaving at least a corner still visible at child height; the children shouldn't have to move anything or climb to be able to spot the heart, but they may have to bend down to look under things. The hearts can be laid down, propped up or Blu-Tacked onto surfaces.
- While they are searching use 'warmer' and 'colder' if the children understand the concept.
- Make sure the children know that they stop looking when they've found one heart.
- The pairs hold hands and sit down to show they have finished.

IDEA

58

Body and Mind

Focus	Group size	Preparation/Resources
Dispositions and Attitudes Self-confidence and Self-esteem Self-care	Any	Clean towels or similar for children to lie on CD/tape player and some gentle background music (optional)

Children take a few moments out of their busy day to lie down and 'let go'.

- Darken the room if possible, and in a calm voice guide the children to lie down carefully on their towel, face-up, and to become aware of their body, relaxing each part in turn, for example: 'Close your eyes gently. Nice and sleepy. Give your toes a little wiggle . . . and stop. Push one knee gently down into the floor . . . then the other . . . Now let your knees go soft . . . Think about your tummy . . . Feel it go up and down as you breathe . . . Listen to the birds outside . . . Stretch your fingers . . . and stop. Listen to the cars going past . . .'
- With practice, children learn to relax quite effectively in this serene atmosphere.

Standing Out in a Crowd

Focus	Group size	Preparation/Resources
Sense of Community	Any	None

Help children to think about the similarities and differences that link them to or distinguish them from 'the crowd'.

- When the children need to line up or group together for any reason, call or send them to the line according to common attributes, e.g. 'If you have black trousers, go and stand by the door . . . If you have buckles/laces/ Velcro on your shoes/a cat at home/like baked beans . . . go and stand over there as well . . .'
- Continue until all the children are accounted for. Children already in the queue gently tap their own head if a later category includes them again.
- Comment on the various groups as they stand up, e.g. 'There are lots of you who have a cat at home', or 'Max, that's very special that you are the only one who has a blue door on your house. Blue is my favourite colour.'

Bye Bye Germs

Focus	Group size	Preparation/Resources
Self-care	Any	Doll (or dolls' house figure, in which case use dolls' house bathroom furniture instead of improvising your own – see next item) Grocery or mailing box large enough to accommodate the doll/cuddly toy/puppet sitting down – this will represent the toilet room Soap, water, a small bowl and a towel or flannel

Children spot the omissions in a doll's toilet visit to reinforce the correct routine.

- Make the box into a toilet cubicle with a door cut into it. Provide a tub or similar to represent the toilet if you wish.
- Tell the children that the doll says she/he can go to the toilet all alone now, without help. Suggest that the children see what the doll does, and if anything is missed out, they can help.
- Check with the children what all the appropriate actions should be and in which order. The correct routine may include: tell an adult you need to 'go'; enter the cubicle and shut the door; (take trousers down, use the toilet, wipe yourself, pull trousers up and flush the toilet); wash and dry hands.
- The doll then shows the children the toilet routine. The five actions bracketed above (takes trousers down . . .) are checked verbally through the toilet door, rather than watched. The doll manages all the points in the right order except washing and drying hands, returning unaware to sit on the adult's lap.
- If necessary prompt the children to pick up on the doll's omission. Wash the doll's hands with real soap and water, then pass it round for the children to check that the hands are clean. Agree it's OK for the doll to eat now, as the germs have been washed away.

SECTION 5   30 – 50 months

This is a stage where self-esteem and confidence need particularly careful nurturing. As children's physical, language and social abilities grow rapidly they need constant support, recognition and praise. They want to be more self-sufficient but feel frustrated if their skills fall short and things don't work out.

They may develop a heightened need for routines and demand for them to be followed rigidly, becoming upset or angry if a detail is changed or omitted.

By around the age of 3 they play imaginatively and cooperatively with other children, becoming increasingly aware of their connection to, and relationships with, other people.

Sit Down and be Counted

Focus	Group size	Preparation/Resources
Dispositions and Attitudes Self-confidence and Self-esteem Sense of Community	Any	Sets of 3–4 pictures/objects to stimulate interest (optional)

Children decide on their own feelings and preferences, while becoming aware that others may make similar or different choices.

- All the children stand up, ready to vote by sitting down as they hear (or see a picture of) their own best answer to a multiple-choice question.
- Ask them, for example:
    - Which animal would you like to be/have in your house [out of these pictured]: tiger, dog, cat or hamster?
    - What would you most like to drive: car, bus, train or tractor?
    - Which activity do you like best: painting, riding sit-on cars, singing or having a story?
    - What would you like to be when you are grown up: fire fighter, postman/lady, taxi driver, baker?
- Children who don't subscribe to any of the categories on offer can say what they would choose and, if possible, why.
- After each question, when all the children are sitting down, select individuals to say why they like whatever it was they chose.

Press Play

Focus	Group size	Preparation/Resources
Dispositions and Attitudes Behaviour and Self-control	Any, according to the size of room available	Oversized TV remote control made from cardboard, with 6 buttons marked: PLAY, STOP, PAUSE, FAST FORWARD, REWIND, EJECT

Children derive enjoyment and gain confidence from mastering a new game or skill. Being physical and quite quick-fire, this game is best played in fairly short bursts.

- Start by teaching the children which actions go with which buttons. The 'buttons' on the pretend remote control are listed below, with the actions listed alongside:

  PLAY: Move your body in a pre-agreed way, e.g. dance, run on the spot.
  STOP: Stop whatever action you're doing.
  PAUSE: Freeze-frame, as in 'musical statues'.
  FAST FORWARD: Scuttle about, using tiny steps.
  REWIND: In slow motion, take two big steps back, having checked empty space behind.
  EJECT: From a curled-up position, pop up and wobble about like a Jack-in-the-box.

- To play the game, children stand in a space of their own. The adult presses a button on the 'remote', then calls out which button has been pressed. The children immediately start the action which belongs to that button, keeping up the same action until a different button is pressed and called out. 'EJECT' marks the end of the game.

Shopping List

Focus	Group size	Preparation/Resources
Dispositions and Attitudes Self-confidence and Self-esteem	Individual or small	List of items for each child who is going 'shopping' Natural jute/cotton shopping bag or similar for each child or pair of children

Children are asked to find common items in the nursery setting. They receive plenty of positive feedback from this fun game, while also gaining a sense of independence.

- Tell the children you need their help with collecting lots of different things. Give each child or pair of children a shopping bag and tell them that everything they need is in this room.
- Ask the children to fetch one or two items at a time and return to you for further instructions, for example: 'Can you find a blue car and a book with an animal on the front?' (Children fetch these items then return for next instruction.) 'Now can you look for three red bricks and a blue teddy?'
- Alternatively, give each child or pair six or seven pictures of items to find from a list, all slightly different, which, if necessary, you help to decipher as they search. Ensure that each child or pair always has a book to find, so they'll be able to sit down and read it if they finish before the others.
- Empty out one completed bag at a time and have all participants help to check off the found items against the items on the list. Stamp or draw a smiley face beside each item that has been produced.
- Say why each child or pair of children did an excellent job – they looked really carefully/didn't give up/finished last but tried for longest.
- After a short play with the items, the children return each one to where they found it.

Taking this further

For older or more confident children include items which involve asking an adult for something, such as a beaker from the kitchen, or arranging to collect something after another child has finished using it, such as a play dough cutter.

Green, Cross Man

Focus	Group size	Preparation/Resources
Making Relationships Behaviour and Self-control	Fairly small, with a ratio of at least 1 adult to 2 children	Cardboard cut-out green man (walking) and red man (standing and facing front)

It is important to familiarize small children with basic road safety rules, even though they are not yet crossing roads unaccompanied.

- When out and about, observe from a safe vantage point the way a puffin crossing works. Explain that when the red man appears on the box beside the pedestrian it means 'stop/don't go'. When the green man is showing, people still need to be sure the traffic has stopped before they step off the kerb.
- Ask the children if they think all the crossing users are following the rules safely.
- Cross the road with the children, following the puffin/pelican rules carefully and stating categorically that although the children are helping you to look, it's you who will decide when you all cross.
- On a different day, introduce the rules for zebra crossings. Make sure the children know that they must wait until the vehicles have completely stopped on both sides before stepping onto the road in case the cars have not seen them and are just slowing down for a nearby turn-off.
- Back at base, play the Green Man game, which is simply STOP (i.e. dancing/ walking/clapping or whatever) when the red man is held up and GO for the green man. You can make the green man 'flash' by turning him round and round to show his uncoloured side/green side (mount him on a pea-stick or piece of dowel and roll the stick back and forth between your hands). He doesn't like it, though, if the children start to 'go' when he is flashing – hence the green, cross man.

Safety note

Because you are going to be near roads, don't take any children on this outing who do not listen well to you, or who will not hold your hand when outside.

Remember that pedestrians waiting at zebra crossings can be hidden in drivers' blind spots.

Abracadabra

Focus	Group size	Preparation/Resources
Self-confidence and Self-esteem Making Relationships	Any	Magic wand (30cm long × 10cm wide piece of thin white card rolled lengthwise into a thin tube, with a shorter, black piece taped over it, leaving white ends protruding)

Children love this game, which encourages them to express their feelings.

- Tell the children you are going to 'magic' them all.
- Use 'Abracadabra' or your own made-up word (e.g. 'Magicata' or someone's name spelt backwards) and 'magic' the children as they stand in a space to: laugh/fall asleep/become cross/cry/think about someone they love/shiver/wear the biggest smile in the whole wide world/jump like a frog/turn to stone/ turn back to happy children again.

We make the Rules

Focus	Group size	Preparation/Resources
Making Relationships Behaviour and Self-control	All the children if possible, as the 'rules' will affect them all	None

Focusing on right and wrong and thinking about the need to take care of others, children help to compile guidelines to make everyone feel safe, happy and cherished.

- Invite anecdotes from the children about anything that has happened to them, particularly in the nursery setting, that made them feel upset or unhappy – but not the names of the culprits.
- Discuss ideas such as: feeling left out or lonely; not being allowed to play; other children not sharing resources; unkind words; hurting or pushing; being too noisy, rough or dangerous.
- Agree simple guidelines on, for example, taking turns and sharing; helping someone who needs you; using the climbing frame sensibly; using words kindly.
- Using the children's own words as far as possible, and illustrating with appropriate pictures, write or type out the guidelines. Display these prominently and refresh them often.
- Praise children when they follow the guidelines.

Bring me Sunshine

Focus	Group size	Preparation/Resources
Sense of Community	Any	None

Teach this poem to help children understand that their body language affects those around them, and that it's lovely to make people smile.

Stamp stamp stamp!
I feel cross!
Wear a frown, oh dear,
Bad day, don't come near!
Jump jump jump!
I feel great!
Laugh and smile, hee, hee, hee!
Good day, play with me.

Show appreciation for children who are naturally happy, and give more serious-minded children plenty of reasons to laugh and smile, to relax and enjoy themselves.

Something in Common

Focus	Group size	Preparation/Resources
Making Relationships Sense of Community	10+, an even number if possible	Pairs of items, e.g. same-shaped or same-coloured bricks; matching cards; matching gloves – make the pairings simple or more complex according to the children's abilities

This simple game encourages manners, cooperation and linking up.

- Teach the children to shake hands with the right hand and to introduce themselves by name, as they will need to do this when they find their 'partner'.
- Distribute randomly all the halves of the pairs of [bricks/cards/gloves] so that every child is holding one half of a pair.
- The children move around carefully, looking for the other child who has the matching pair to their object. They then say their names, shake hands and sit down, ready to show their completed pair when all the children have found their pairs.
- Be ready to sort out mismatches quickly so that everyone can complete the game.

IDEA

69

Listen While You Work

Focus	Group size	Preparation/Resources
Sense of Community	Any	Music in a range of cultural styles, perhaps loaned by families CD/tape player

Introduce children to a variety of musical cultures and invite their responses.

- Play different styles of music on different days as background while the children are busy with fairly quiet activities, or have them rest for a few minutes and listen purposefully to the music.
- Ask the children for their reactions. In the absence of volunteers, select any children who seemed particularly to respond to the music. Keeping the music playing softly, find out:
  - Do they think the music is happy/fast/sad?
  - Does the music make them feel calm/sleepy?
  - Does it make them play or move more quickly?
  - Do they like it/not like it?
  - Would they like it played in their house at bed time/while they're getting ready for nursery?
- Encourage the children to move to the music. Do they feel happy/sad/ sleepy/spikey/far away?
- Leave the music playing for a little while after discussing the children's responses, so that they can listen again in the light of any new thoughts.

Interesting Family

Focus	Group size	Preparation/Resources
Sense of Community	Any	Contact parents for any interesting information about significant family members

It is interesting for children to realize that certain people can pop up in more than one context, connecting different parts of their lives.

- Gather information from parents regarding any member of their family who in their working lives might meet or influence the children, such as an aunt who's a local policewoman. You may be able to borrow photos or a simple diary about their working day or they may come and talk to the children.
- Ask the children what they think these people might do in the course of their work. Tie in what they say with any details you have been given by the family.
- If possible, relay snippets of information about the relative's home life as well. Children will be interested to hear that their friend Jennie's uncle, who works in the greengrocer's on the corner and sells fruit and vegetables to their own family, has a parrot that says, 'What have you done, you bad boy?', when he comes in from work.

We Do That in Our House Too

Focus	Group size	Preparation/Resources
Sense of Community	Any	None

This idea helps to generate awareness and respect for cultural differences in families.

- Using questions which show interest without being intrusive, invite the children to feed back their different versions of the routine in question, such as: getting ready for bed; helping parents with jobs around the home; laying the table and eating a family meal; shopping for food or clothes; having breakfast.
- Try to ensure that the children listen to one another.
- Recap every so often to contrast routines in different homes, e.g. 'Adya's special job is helping her mummy every day to tidy the house. Thomas helps by putting his toys away when his bedroom gets in a mess.'

Put it in the Bin

Focus	Group size	Preparation/Resources
Behaviour and Self-control	Small to medium, with usual adult to child ratio for outings	Clipboard, pencil and paper A pre-visit on the day if possible

It's never too soon to raise awareness of green issues, so take the children rubbish-spotting in the park or other open space.

- Before the walk, talk to the children about the sort of rubbish they are likely to see and why litter bins are there.
- On the walk, adults act as scribes to record all the different types of litter the children have spotted. Make the walk long enough to convey the message that litter looks dirty and is unacceptable.
- Read back the litter list to the children and impress on them that every person who dropped litter has contributed to making a mess of the park.
- Ask the children to think about always putting litter in the bin or taking it home to recycle.

Taking this further

If appropriate to the age/ability of the children, discuss the biodegradable nature of some litter and the dangers of plastic rubbish to wildlife.

Don't Chase the Pigeons!

Focus	Group size	Preparation/Resources
Behaviour and Self-control	Any	None

This may take the form of a follow-on to the previous activity ('Put it in the Bin') to teach children why they should be considerate towards all living things.

- Tell the story of some children who are playing happily in the park and are frightened by a big barking dog which is running around them.
- Tell the children another story from the point of view of an animal or bird that is being chased by some children. Highlight the feelings of the helpless creatures – the same fear and upset felt by the children in the first story.
- Invite reactions from the children to both stories.
- Emphasize that in both stories the 'attackers' were only playing, but didn't think about the consequences or the feelings of their victim; in each case they were being unkind to a smaller or weaker being.

Taking this further

If animals could talk, how would they ask us to behave towards them? Try compiling a list of the children's ideas for animals' 'rules'.

IDEA 74

What a Mess

Focus	Group size	Preparation/Resources
Making Relationships Behaviour and Self-control	Any	Large box of plastic bricks or similar

A staged 'accident' gives children a chance to see that they are able to help others.

- Just before or during tidy-up time, arrange for an adult to 'accidentally' tip over a large box of plastic bricks, the more mess, the better.
- Wait for or invite individual children to assist with picking up the bricks.
- If there are enough already helping, direct further volunteers to a different worthwhile job, such as sweeping up sand.
- During circle time, praise all the children who helped, saying how good it was for the adult not to be picking up the bricks/sweeping sand on their own, how kind it was that the children helped, and how much quicker the job was done.
- Give all willing children a chance to help with a job as soon as possible, praising them all roundly.

IDEA
75

Promise Presents

Focus	Group size	Preparation/Resources
Making Relationships Behaviour and Self-control Sense of Community	Any	Small empty boxes, e.g. for tea bags, chocolates Wrapping paper – neutral style, e.g. stars/plain/ spotted Sticky tape Hand-made gift cards or tags to write the promise on

The children wrap a parcel that will never be opened, because the gift is actually a promise, written on the label.

- Each child selects an empty box and the wrapping paper they think their recipient would like, then has help with wrapping the box.
- Help each child to decide on a promise they feel able to keep (some children's ideas below), and write it on the card or tag for them. Suggest they fulfil the promise as soon as they can, in case they forget it.
- The children present the gifts to their special person.

Promises could include:

- to wash the car
- to be good
- to help Daddy find his keys
- to play with my sister
- to stop eating crisps.

The Curly Hair Club

Focus	Group size	Preparation/Resources
Sense of Community	Medium to large	Large, strong box, e.g. from a big television or freezer, open side uppermost and a door cut in another side so that the children can step into it (a box gives better entertainment value, but if unavailable, use an off-cut of clean carpet about 1m × 1m) Whistle or hand bell (optional)

This game draws attention to the similarities between people, helping children to see that we always have something to bond us together.

- Children walk around the box (or carpet square) using all available space.
- The adult calls out (and rings a bell/blows a whistle), 'Time for . . . The Curly Hair Club!' All the children with curly hair have to step inside the box. All the children outside call, 'Hello Curly Hair Club!' to which they answer, 'Hello!'
- Repeat, trying, 'Time for . . . The Walk to School Club/Cat and Dog Club (like/own a cat or dog)/Black Shoes Club/Hate Chips Club/Three Years Old Club/Green is Our Favourite Colour Club.'
- Point out, if you can, that the children outside the box also have something in common, such as all being 4 years old.
- It obviously helps to know your children well and to choose the 'club' titles with a mind for the capacity of the box or carpet. In cases of unexpected over-subscription, have the children take turns in groups to fill the box, or bring together in the box the few children who are *not* in the club.

Safety note

At least one adult should stand by the box to ensure that it remains stable when the children are in it.

IDEA

77

Banana

Focus	Group size	Preparation/Resources
Making Relationships	Small to medium	None

Laughter is a great tonic, and this silly game ensures that children relax and enjoy the company of the other children and adults.

- With the children sitting in a circle, work your way round either randomly or methodically, asking each child a simple question in a serious tone of voice. Ideas include:

  '[Mario], have I got something on my nose?'
  '[Gracie], what's your mummy's name?'
  '[Duncan], what's that you're wearing on your feet?'
  '[Nita], what do you sleep on at night?'

- The answer, agreed in advance, is the same for each child in the circle: choose something like 'banana', 'sausages', 'fish finger', or 'mashed potato', all of which produce humour and usually work well. Save unused responses for replaying the game another day.
- Help children to join in with any laughter that arises as a result of what they have said, and to understand that they are not being laughed *at*.

IDEA 78

Traditions

Focus	Group size	Preparation/Resources
Sense of Community	Any	Ask the children's families to provide stories (and photos/artefacts if possible) about how they welcome/name a new baby in their families

With this activity children learn to understand and respect that people observe special events in different ways.

- Share and discuss the stories you have collected from families regarding special baby ceremonies. These ceremonies may be religious or non-religious.
- If parents have loaned artefacts, there will be links from these to some lovely creative work, such as sponging through paper doilies to produce lacy patterns which echo the lace seen on a christening gown, or making little foil-covered, decorated bands to represent the steel bracelets given to Sikh babies.
- The children may like to act out the following Sikh baby-naming ceremony, or any other that takes their imagination and is practicable. The Guru Granth Sahib (the book of holy verses) is opened at random and the first letter of the reading becomes the initial of the baby's name. The baby is given a steel bracelet to wear as a sign of their faith.

IDEA 79

No Two Alike

Focus	Group size	Preparation/Resources
Making Relationships	Any	None
Behaviour and Self-control		
Sense of Community		

Children are encouraged to welcome differences between people.

- Discuss how everybody looks and is different. If you have identical twins in the group, discuss how they differ from each other, for example with regard to personality and preferences.
- Make sure the children understand that each one of them is special, and praise each child for something special they have done, for example: 'I think your idea for the car game was really good and your friends had lots of fun playing it with you' (implying that the child is innovative and well liked); or 'I saw you cuddling your friend when he was crying and I think that was a really kind thing to do' (implying that the child is kind and thoughtful and has a close friend).
- Convey the message that it's good to get to know 'new' people or play with them to find out what they are like and how they are special. We often find they are kind or funny or good at something surprising. If we reject them on the basis of first impressions we could miss out on new friends.

 Taking this further

For older children, you might like to touch on racial and cultural issues, disabilities and physical appearance. Remind the children that we need to look at the person not the label.

IDEA 80

With a Little Help from My Friends

Focus	Group size	Preparation/Resources
Dispositions and Attitudes	Any, with the usual adult to child ratio for outings	Clipboard, pencil and paper for each group Simple bar chart or similar to record the pooled findings (optional)

Working collaboratively, children gain experience at tackling a challenge.

- Choose a question to research, such as, 'Who uses the park on Wednesdays?' Alternatively, explore whether a statement is true or false, such as, 'People walk their dogs only in the afternoon.'
- Tell the children they are going to conduct a survey in the park. Ask them to predict what they might find with regard to the selected question.
- In the park, sit everyone down somewhere clean and with a good view. Give small groups a subject to count, such as mums or dads/mums and dads with pushchairs; dog walkers; cyclists; young people playing sports. Try to ensure that all the children look hard for at least some of the time.
- If they are able, the children take turns within their group to keep tally while their counterparts do the spotting. Teach the five-bar gate method (卌) if appropriate. Alternatively, an adult in each group can scribe, explaining to the children how they are doing it.
- Try to survey more than one part of the park to obtain a fair picture.
- Back at base, children help to use the findings to answer the original question.
- Transfer the findings to the bar chart if appropriate.

Safety note
Remind children not to touch their faces until hands are well washed after the park trip.

SECTION 6 — 40 – 60+ months

Around this age and with self-confidence increasing, children start to become emotionally more self-sufficient. They begin to be more social, often able to share their toys or wait for a turn without being prompted. Play is cooperative and imaginative. At the same time, children start to enjoy their own company.

During this stage they become fervently aware of what is fair, and of rules and codes of behaviour; this can result in their taking a firm opposite stance and then being difficult to sway.

Children of 4 and 5 often show sensitivity and may develop a touching concern for someone's upset or injury, but may also be *in*sensitive, even unkind, towards others.

We Don't Mind Being Out

Focus	Group size	Preparation/Resources
All six aspects	Medium/large	Large plastic hula hoops or large carpet samples

Playing the game 'Shipwreck' helps children learn to feel comfortable with not winning, and with being 'out'.

Shipwreck: how to play
- Allowing one hoop to three or four children to begin with, spread the hoops around the floor. The hoops represent the islands; the area around them is the sea.
- The children move around the hoops sedately, as if on ships, until you call 'Shipwreck!' at which point they head for any of the hoops. Tell the children to stand facing out, so that if they are pushed by mistake they can step forwards instead of tripping over the hoop backwards.
- Remove one hoop after each shipwreck cycle, until when you call 'Shipwreck!' the islands start to overflow. Those without two feet in the hoop are considered 'out', and they become the 'watchers' to make sure the game is played well. The adult's decision is final as to who is out.
- Emphasize that there will be another chance for those who are 'out' to play again in a few minutes or on another day. Consult them in some way so that they still feel included, e.g. 'How many hoops are left now?' or ask them to keep an eye on the removed hoops so that the other children don't use them by mistake.

A Queue for You

Focus	Group size	Preparation/Resources
Making Relationships Behaviour and Self-control	Any	None

Children are encouraged to think about the implications of not waiting fairly for a turn.

- Tell a story about a little girl whose grandmother gave her money to buy an ice cream from the van. After waiting for *ages* because other children and grown-ups kept pushing in front of her, she finally found herself at the front of the queue, only to be told by the man that he was sorry but he'd run out of ice cream. Because she was tired from standing there so long, and because she had no ice cream after such a long wait, the little girl felt like crying.
- Discuss the children's responses to the story, and talk about: who could have helped her to avoid this happening and how; how queuing works and why a queue is more fair (first come, first served).
- Talk about examples such as bus stops, supermarkets and cinemas and ask the children what they think happened next in the story.
- Act out the story with a sad ending, and again but with a happier outcome.

IDEA

83

Pass it On

Focus	Group size	Preparation/Resources
Behaviour and Self-control Sense of Community	Medium to large	None

This helps children to understand that their actions and body language have an effect on others.

- Sit the children in a circle.
- The children silently pass a friendly hand-squeeze around the circle, looking at the recipient as they do so.
- Compare the effects of the hand squeeze to the effects of a hard stare passed round the circle.
- Finish with a positive action, such as passing a smile around.
- The action may be passed on each time to the child immediately to the left or right. Better eye contact can be made, however, if each 'giver' crosses the circle and kneels in front of another child to pass on the action. Each child places their hands on their own knees, or does any agreed action to show that they have had a turn.

Positive and Negative

Focus	Group size	Preparation/Resources
Making Relationships	Any	None
Behaviour and Self-control		

Children are asked to make simple judgements – positive or negative – about a series of minor events.

- Agree a particular pair of signs to denote positive and negative responses, e.g. thumbs up/thumbs down; nodding/shaking head.
- Reel off a series of positive/negative scenarios or a story in which, say Billy, has mixed fortunes during his day (suggestions below). The children 'accompany' the story with the agreed signs, deciding whether they consider each event to be positive or negative.
- Discuss the 'rights and wrongs', 'good and bad' of Billy's day as perceived by the children. Be ready to accept surprising judgements, especially if the children can justify their choices.

Billy's story

Billy woke up today and fell out of bed . . . onto his duvet which had slipped onto the floor . . . He brushed his teeth . . . jumped down four stairs at a time . . . shouted at his baby brother . . . spat out his cornflakes . . . washed up his bowl . . . gave his brother a cuddle . . .

IDEA 85

Here Comes the Bride

Focus	Group size	Preparation/Resources
Sense of Community	Any	Box with dressing-up clothes themed for multicultural weddings Samples of wedding-style food or ingredients to make them Ask parents for photos and accounts of family weddings, including music, food traditions and recipes if possible

During a themed week or over a longer period, children are introduced to various wedding traditions and can dress up and sample wedding fare.

- Depending on the number of different ethnic groups represented in your setting, and on the type of artefacts loaned by families, the wedding theme can be spread over a number of days.
- If parents are able to loan CDs of music that is typically played at weddings, use these as background while the children dress up as brides, grooms, attendants and guests. Stage a mini-wedding ceremony if children are keen.
- Produce some of the wedding food for the children to sample, or the children themselves can assemble pre-cooked or simple food to provide a wedding breakfast, with tables dressed appropriately.
- Discuss the significance of the various traditions practised by all the different families.

IDEA 86

Budding Poets

Focus	Group size	Preparation/Resources
Dispositions and Attitudes Self-confidence and Self-esteem	Any	Whiteboard or large sheet of paper to draft the poem

Everybody works together to create a poem, which is then taken home and 'read' to parents.

- Using as many of the children's ideas as possible, write a collective poem (e.g. 'Cats' – see below). Aim for a consensus of ideas/choice of words so that all the children feel involved. Remember that the poem does not have to rhyme.
- Help the children to learn the completed poem by heart. Write it up and print off a copy for each of the children. It's then illustrated by them and taken home, where it can be recited or 'read' to their families.

Cats
One black cat looking through the window
Two ginger cats lying in the sun
Three Siamese cats slurping up their dinner
Four silly cats standing in the rain
Five stripey cats chasing round the garden
Six black and white cats swishing tails.

The poem can of course be more, or less ambitious according to age and ability.

All Change!

Focus	Group size	Preparation/Resources
Making Relationships Behaviour and Self-control Sense of Community	4–8	Enough small but interesting toys for half of the group

This is all about playing – and living – in peace and harmony.

- Discuss sharing and taking turns, asking children for examples from their experience. Remind them that we sometimes need to pass on or give up something we're still enjoying ourselves.
- With the children sitting in a circle, give about two-thirds of the group an appealing toy each, telling them to play with it in the circle and explaining that everybody will have a turn soon.
- Ask each of the children without a toy, which toy they would like to play with. Encourage them to ask if they may have a turn in a minute, and then to wait without 'crowding' the child who's finishing a turn.
- Welcome negotiations – for example, the original child with the toy may ask to have it back for another turn when the second or third child has finished with it.
- Draw attention to and praise the use of words such as 'please', 'thank you', 'sorry'. Try to ensure that the children carry out promises, such as to return a toy or to have only a quick go.
- Calmly repeat your sharing 'code' if you have to sort out any refusals or squabbles.

IDEA

88

Zig-Zag Books

Focus	Group size	Preparation/Resources
Behaviour and Self-control	Any	White- or pastel-coloured A4 card, cut lengthwise, then each strip folded into 3, making 2 zig-zag books per A4 sheet of card

Focusing on living things, children record ways of caring for their favourite animal.

- Discuss what care is given to pets at the children's homes, namely feeding, watering, housing and bedding, cleanliness, grooming, exercise, vet visits and medicines and, not forgetting, loving.
- Help the children complete the zig-zag books with reference to their favourite pet (actual or desired), one aspect of care to a page. Provide line drawings for the children to copy as required or photocopy pictures/ drawings to cut and paste.
- Use one of the pages to write in the name of the pet.

Cleanliness

Focus	Group size	Preparation/Resources
Behaviour and Self-control Self-care	Small (groups could be rotated on different days)	Dustpan and brush Clean cloth, washing-up liquid and warm water 'Dirty' cloth (see below)

Children enjoy helping to make things clean and sparkling, and it makes sense for them to learn at an early age about germs and hygiene.

- At tidy-up time, ask several children to help sweep up the floor and wash the table that was used for play dough. Ask them if this yucky old cloth (made up with brown/grey paint to look dirty but otherwise clean and not germ-ridden) will do the job, trying to elicit ideas that it would add germs and not really clean the table.
- Ask if they think a clean cloth and just water will clean the table well. Compare it with washing our hands and bodies without soap.
- Look at the 'before and after' effect when half the table has been cleaned with a few drops of washing-up liquid, warm water and a clean cloth.
- Explain that germs smell bad. Smell the clean table!
- Help the cleaning group feed back findings to the rest of the children.

IDEA 90

We Belong Together

Focus	Group size	Preparation/Resources
Dispositions and Attitudes Self-confidence and Self-esteem Making Relationships	3+	Ball of chunky multicoloured wool

A ball of wool is unravelled as it passes from person to person in the circle, linking all the children together as they reflect on personal questions.

- With the children sitting calmly and comfortably in a circle, tell them, 'Today we are going to think about who we love. When the ball of wool is given to you, hold it and say the name of the person you love. It's OK if you just want to think about the person instead of saying their name: just say, "I'm thinking about her/him." Then pass the ball to the person on the other side of you.'
- Start the ball rolling by saying who you love (and maybe why), before holding on to the beginning of the wool and passing the ball to the child beside you, allowing the wool to unravel.
- After speaking, each child keeps holding on to the length of wool until everyone has spoken.
- On another day, try, 'The person I want to say thank you to is . . .' or, on a less personal level, 'My favourite story is . . .'

IDEA

91

Poor Old Ted

Focus	Group size	Preparation/Resources
Behaviour and Self-control	Any	Teddy

This helps children to understand that both positive and negative words and actions have consequences for others.

- Tell children that poor Teddy is sad. Because he is shy and doesn't like talking, nobody plays with him/he's been told he's stupid/he's been called Smelly Teddy. Sensitively make links with any troubles recently encountered by children in your care.
- Either ask the children for ideas about what Teddy should do or say, and who he could ask for help, or pass him round the circle for each child to give him positive advice, a cuddle and/or some kind words.

Some People Want it All

Focus	Group size	Preparation/Resources
Making Relationships	Any	Plate of apple slices or fruit, with enough pieces to offer to every participating adult and child, with a couple of pieces left over

This reinforces the importance of sharing.

- Hold the plate of apple slices and tell the children you are very hungry. Nobody else has anything to eat.
- Ask the children if any of them are hungry too.
- Ask for ideas about:
  - whether the fruit should be shared. If so, why?
  - what you should say to the children ('Would anyone like..?')
  - what you will do if there aren't enough slices for everyone to have a piece (cut some slices into smaller pieces).
- Go round and offer the plate for everyone to take a piece. Encourage children to take the piece nearest them, and praise those who remember to say 'Thank you'. You could eat the leftover slices yourself if there are only one or two (do the children think that fair?), or offer them round again if there are enough.
- When the apple slices are finished, play a little favourite game or sing a song, simply enjoying each other's company.
- Tell everyone that you enjoyed sharing and having a little 'apple party' with them.

IDEA
93

Snowflakes, Wheels and Sweepers

Focus	Group size	Preparation/Resources
Dispositions and Attitudes Self-confidence and Self-esteem Making Relationships	12+	Christmassy or wintery music (optional)

This game requires plenty of cooperation and flexibility.

- Divide the children into three groups and give each group a particular movement to perform, namely:
    - 'Wheels' hold hands in a circle and walk round very slowly, facing in.
    - 'Sweepers' walk slowly forwards across the room in a straight line, holding hands.
    - 'Snowflakes' are individuals who can stick to the 'wheels' or be pushed along by the 'sweepers'.
- Play the music if you are using it.
- The snowflakes stand with the main adult. Wheels and sweepers start up their special movements. When the sweepers reach a wall, they stop and let go of each others' hands, then turn round and re-form before setting off slowly in the opposite direction.
- When the adult calls 'It's snowing!' the snowflakes flutter about and land where they can, either holding the joined hands of the wheels, or walking in step in front of the sweepers. Now as they turn, the wheels have to be careful not to let the snowflakes fall off, and the sweepers and snowflakes must move forward gently without tripping over one another.
- When the adult calls 'Melting!' the snowflakes slip away and stand back with the adult.
- Everybody changes roles to play once or twice more.

Taking this further
Before the 'snow' arrives, tell the wheel it's just hit a bump and goes all wobbly, or tell the sweepers to jump up and down to shake dust off. The children have to try and coordinate their movements.

Old Mrs Lacey

Focus	Group size	Preparation/Resources
Making Relationships Behaviour and Self-control Sense of Community	Any	None

Children are encouraged to think about the needs of the elderly and how everybody can help them.

- Play the game 'Old Mrs Lacey'.

  Say: 'Old Mrs Lacey is coming to tea' and the children, standing, respond: 'What's she like?'
  'Well, she has a bad leg (pretend to hobble forward a step)/can't see well (hand across forehead as if looking into sun)/can't hear very well (cup hand behind ear)/keeps forgetting things' ('tut-tut' and shake head). As well as realistic afflictions, mix in humorous touches such as 'she wrinkles up her nose/sings in the bath (la-la-la-laaah)'.

- The game is played cumulatively, i.e. the children mimic the original action first, then add on all subsequent actions in order, while you repeat the appropriate words. Prompt the children if necessary, so that they always arrive at the correct sequence.
- Ask the children how they would look after Mrs Lacey if she came to tea at their house, e.g. avoid bumping into her bad leg/fetch things to save her walking/describe things to her that she can't see/look at her while speaking clearly/help her remember things, and be patient when she's forgetful.

IDEA

95

Little Monkey!

Focus	Group size	Preparation/Resources
Behaviour and Self-control	Any	Monkey toy or puppet

This idea invites the children to think about negative behaviour and the need for boundaries.

- Animate the puppet or toy, making it misbehave during story time. Make it: punch an adult, keep interrupting, knock things down, throw things, hide under a chair, cover its ears and refuse to listen.
- Ask the children what they think of the puppet's behaviour. What do they want to say to him? What should the puppet say now? Ask him if he's sorry. (Puppet nods and looks sorry.) What should he do now? (Help to tidy up his mess/sit quietly during the story.)
- Praise all the children and the puppet for listening to the story so well. Make sure it's a good story!

IDEA

96

In your Burrow!

Focus	Group size	Preparation/Resources
Self-confidence and Self-esteem Making Relationships Behaviour and Self-control	Medium or large	Lightweight cloth large enough to completely cover a curled- up child Large room is needed

This game involves all the children in getting to know one another better and is best played when everyone already knows many or most of the other children's names.

Explain the game to the children.

- All of the children are little rabbits. They have a lovely time, running and skipping in the fields together, but they must be careful not to let the farmer see them.
- When you see the farmer coming, you shout, 'Farmer's coming! Hide, little rabbits!' at which point the rabbits quickly curl up on their knees on the floor, arms folded over their heads and eyes shut tightly, pretending to be hiding down a burrow.
- Cover just one of the hiding rabbits with the cloth. (Demonstrate this before the game on a volunteer or two, and check with them that it feels OK to be covered for a short time. In the game itself this usually works out no longer than about one minute, and most children are quite happy being the covered-up rabbit.)
- When you say, 'Farmer's gone now, come out little rabbits!' all the children stand up *except* the one covered by the cloth.
- Select a child to say the name of which rabbit is missing, i.e. the name of the child under the cloth, still hiding. So that the child under the cloth doesn't get too tired or hot when nobody guesses correctly, start giving clues such as 'It's a [girl] rabbit'/'Rabbit is wearing a Superman t-shirt'/ 'Rabbit wears glasses.'
- Before saying who they think it is, children should be encouraged to check that the person they are thinking of is not already out of their burrow and standing there large as life.
- The child who first guesses correctly can either be applauded, or can help you with covering a rabbit the next time round.

Birdie Song

Focus	Group size	Preparation/Resources
Behaviour and Self-control Self-care	Any	Ingredients for bird seed cake (seed, cake crumbs, lard)

This rhyme tells children how important it is to leave food out for the birds, especially in cold weather.

• Make a bird seed cake with the children and position it where you can watch the birds feeding. (Once you've attracted the birds, remember to keep feeding them throughout the year.)
• When the cold weather approaches, teach the children the following words either as a poem, or sing to the tune of 'Kookaburra sits in the old gum tree':

Little robin sits in the snowy tree,
Very very cold outside is he. (hug yourself and tremble with cold)
Come, little robin, (beckon)
Here, little robin, (beckon again)
You'll be fed by me. (point to yourself)

This sounds lovely and Christmassy with a tambour and/or sleigh bells played sparingly.

IDEA 98

Agony Aunts and Uncles

Focus	Group size	Preparation/Resources
Self-care	Any	Toy or puppet (Monkey or similar)

Children are asked to give advice to Monkey to help him out of trouble.

- Tell the children that Monkey has hurt his foot/banged his head/lost his dad in the supermarket/heard his nan is poorly.
- How do the children think Monkey is feeling? What does he need to help him feel better or to resolve the problem? Whom should he ask for help and what should he say to them?
- The children draw on their own experiences, such as being lost in a shop, to give Monkey some practical advice.

The children's responses can give useful insights into their lives and into the way they think.

Taking this further

This activity could lead to some role play/improvised drama. It's preferable to cover one scenario at a time, perhaps as a daily or weekly slot when Monkey's current problems are sorted out.

Run, Rabbit, Run

Focus	Group size	Preparation/Resources
Dispositions and Attitudes Self-confidence and Self-esteem	Medium	None

This game encourages children to link up to others in a time of need, so that they feel secure.

- The adult demonstrates the following sequence. Start with the left hand, held flat, palm down, level with your neck. Cover left hand with the right hand, then pull out the left and replace it on top of the right, and so on. Always keep your hands level with your chin.
  As you do this, say:
  'Run, rabbit,
  Run rabbit,
  Run,
  Run,
  Run.'
  Each new line should matching another hand movement. After the last 'Run', fold your arms wordlessly.
- With the children seated in a circle, their task is to take turns to copy, one by one, exactly what you have shown them. If they get everything completely right, including folding their arms, congratulate them and move on to the next child in the circle. If they forget anything (usually the folding arms even when they've mastered the hands and the rhyme), just say, 'Don't worry. Have another go in a minute', and move on to the next child's turn.
- If that's all there were to the game, you'd quickly have a number of disgruntled children on your hands, convinced they were doing it right but not realizing they had to fold their arms to complete the sequence, so . . .
  if nobody 'gets it' on the first round, and before frustration sets in, give any extra hint you feel is necessary to help some of the children to complete the sequence correctly. These children then support and, if necessary, coach the others, talking them through it until everyone has cracked it.
- Finish on a rendering of the whole thing in unison, with folding arms to complete the sequence perfectly.

Candle Light

Focus	Group size	Preparation/Resources
Sense of Community	Any	Large, stable candle, preferably in a storm jar or similar CD or tape of peaceful, atmospheric music or natural sounds Pictures or artefacts relating to the ways that light is used in religious settings around the world, such as Advent, Diwali, Hanukah (optional)

This activity focuses on the spiritual nature of light, particularly candle light.

- Discuss any pictures or religious artefacts you have, to illustrate how light and candle light are used in different religious lives around the world.
- Tell the children that candles help to make people feel peaceful and to think about how they can be good, kind and helpful.
- With the room darkened as much as possible and music playing softly, light the big candle and encourage the children to relax, concentrating on the light all around the candle.
- Ask the children to think of something they can do today that is good or kind or helpful. Ask them to think quietly about how they will do that and who will be pleased they have done it. Emphasize that they don't tell anybody, just think it in their heads.
- Enjoy the candlelit peace.

Safety note

A few important reminders about candle safety:

- **Strike any matches well away from the children or, better still, light the candle with a taper.**
- **Make sure the candle is stable and can't be knocked over, staying with it at all times.**
- **Use a snuffer to extinguish the flame.**